$MAKING $ense OF IT ALL

Making $ense of it All

Ten Financial Principles for a Better Financial Future

James Giuliani, CFA, CFP® and CPA

5 | *Points*
Publishing

5Points Publishing
A Dunham Books imprint
63 Music Square East
Nashville, Tennessee 37203

Trade Paperback ISBN: 978-1-939447-09-8
Ebook ISBN: 978-1-939447-10-4

Printed in the United States of America

To the One for which
my life and this book
would not be possible:
Jesus Christ.

Table of Contents

Introduction

I am so excited you picked up this book because I am relatively certain that you will learn at least one thing you didn't know before, and that one thing will be powerful enough to impact your financial future. It is that very thought that fueled me to pursue three vigorous financial designations and put my heart and soul into writing this book. As unbelievable as it may sound, you were in mind every time I opened up a textbook in preparation for various financial certification examinations; the ultimate goal was for all that knowledge to make its way into a book, which is now in your hands! At the core of this book is a deep desire for every reader to connect with something that will get them to change their financial trajectory. Planning our financial future can be a very scary undertaking in any economic environment and it may be even more so as we come out of the recent "Great Recession." It is so easy to leave the planning to the experts or to chance it and just pray that you will come out okay on the other side. However, many of you have purchased this book declaring that it is no longer good enough to rely on chance.

Secondly, my goal with this book was to put it in plain language that does not require a team of lawyers to understand. I want this book to be fun. I want it to be fun to talk about budgeting and planning for your retirement. The letters next to my name on the cover are only so you can have confidence in my message and for me to establish needed credibility. I want you to buy in to the message of this book for it to make a difference in your life. For me personally, I feel more secure when I know that the speaker or author is qualified enough to deliver their message. We live in a complex world that requires expert help at times. However, there are some fundamental financial concepts that we can all understand and implement. I think in this country and in this world, there is a lack of exposure to financial concepts and a lack of strong passion for the topic of financial planning. I do not think this is because people lack the ability to understand financial concepts. This is a key point. I meet people all the time that become uncomfortable when the topic of finances comes up in a conversation. Some of them resort to platitudes or clichés ("rules of thumb") that they have heard in passing or saw on the elevator screen in their office building. We can be so much better! There is a better way, and this book is focused on putting financial concepts in a format that lessens some of the discomfort financial planning causes us. My goal is to give you the confidence and knowledge to plan for your financial future. Given that, this book is divided into Ten Financial Principles, with each chapter touching on a principle that if followed, could have an immediate impact on your life.

Lastly, you will notice at times in this book that biblical references are made. My hope is that you will be open-minded enough about your financial freedom that a few such references do not cause you to disregard important financial principles and continue with the status quo. This book is absolutely not about how God is going to make you rich and solve all your financial problems. I have intentionally made this book as relevant and relatable to as many people as possible. Any biblical element to this book is primarily included because it is a principle that I believe has universal truth. This book gleans from my experience in the financial arena, and given there is a personal aspect to that, there will be some themes that I use simply because they speak about my personal experience in certain areas. This is most prevalent, for example, in the charity section. I truly believe that the charity section of the book can not only have a major impact on others' financial lives but also on our own. Personal examples can be more powerful, credible, and motivating than pages upon pages of boring financial information. I intentionally avoided writing this book like a textbook. When you go to the bookstore (do they still have those anymore?), you don't get mad at the bookstore for having a few books you don't want to read. You just walk by those shelves and look for the book you want. I would approach this book in the same way. Not every concept is going to be meaningful to you, but many will. So don't let a few sentences stop you from seeing the big picture, which is making a better financial future for you and those you love.

Tax Planning Principles

Taxes are one of those realities we all must face. It would be great to actually receive our full salary or all of the profit before taxes if we own a business, while at the same time enjoying driving on interstates and generally living in a country where we have our freedom. The reality of the situation is that we live in a free country and there is a price (in the form of taxation) to keeping it that way. There are certainly trade-offs and much debate over how much we should pay in taxes, but that is well beyond the scope of this discussion and not something I could probably answer even if this book focused on that topic. However we are certain of one thing—taxes are something we are going to deal with for the rest of our lives. As you will find out later in this book, even in death we get taxed via an estate tax. This section will focus on the tax most popular and relevant to United States residents: U.S. federal income tax. If you live in a different country, your specific tax situation will differ, but you will still benefit from this chapter as tax fundamentals share certain commonalities across tax jurisdictions. All attempts were made to use the latest tax guidance as of the publication date of this book. Tax formulas, deductions, and other rules are courtesy of the Internal Revenue Code ("IRC"). Refer to the Internal Revenue Service ("IRS") website to ensure you are aware of any updates from the date of this publication. This section attempts to take the tax rules as promulgated by the IRC and explain these rules in a more approachable terminology.

Introduction to U.S. Federal Income Tax

U.S. federal income tax and state income tax (if your state has income tax) have a lot of similarities, so we will primarily focus on federal income tax, which is the bigger number. The principals learned in this section will also help you manage your state tax liability. There are items that are taxed for federal purposes but not state purposes and vice versa, so it is important to be aware that differences exist. Typically, your state tax return will list out the adjustments that need to be made to your federal taxable income. Your state will also supply tax instructions that will make identification of these items easier.

The best way to think about income tax is that everything you earn or attain is taxable, unless the IRC says it is not taxable. A common question I get is: "Do I need to report this item on my tax return?" The simple answer is also a question: "Does the IRC specifically state that it is exempt from being reported on your tax return?" The IRC already has enough volume as it is, so to try and list every piece of income that is taxable would be an exhaustive undertaking. This is a very broad starting point, but it is crucial to understanding your taxes. Secondly, your taxable income is a gross number. What this means is that it includes everything you earn, even if you break even after expenses. For example, if you receive $100 from a home business and have $100 of expenses, you would still report the $100 of taxable income. The $100 of expenses could be fully, partially, or not deductible, and there is a section on your tax return to report this information, but the gross receipts must be listed first. I will discuss how to report various types of expenses on your tax return in greater detail later in this chapter, as you will need to determine whether you can deduct certain expenses.

Determining How You Want to File

An important consideration to make regarding taxes is how you want to file. If you are a single person, your decision will be pretty easy; you will file your tax return as a single filer. If you are married, you will have the option to file jointly or separately, with married filing jointly generally being the preferable way from a tax savings perspective. There are also special circumstances that will allow you to file as a head of household or a qualified widow. These different distinctions will dictate which tax brackets your income falls into, dollar values where deductions start to phase out, and the dollar amount of your standard deduction.

How to Calculate the Taxes You Owe

The first step in calculating your tax is calculating your income. Determining what qualifies as income is pretty straightforward. Rarely does the IRC exclude income from the taxable income calculation. Rather, it is more common for the IRC to instead provide various deductions (both before calculating adjusted gross income and after adjusted gross income) that can be taken on the tax return to reduce the taxable income number. You may be thinking, "Slow down man, what do you mean adjusted gross income?" I am glad you asked!

Per the IRC, Adjusted Gross Income ("AGI") is the result of taking your gross income, which is all the income you earned during the year (that is not specifically excluded for tax purposes) and subtracting any "before AGI" deductions that you may have.

Before AGI deductions are listed in the IRC, and examples include expenses like:

- Qualified moving costs;
- Contributions to a Health Savings Account ("HSA");
- Student loan interest;
- IRA contributions; and
- Personal business expenses (assuming the business qualifies as a true business and not a hobby—more on that later).

These are powerful deductions because they impact your AGI, and AGI is used as a threshold for determining whether you are eligible to receive all, some, or none of certain "after AGI" deductions. Specifically, certain deductions are disallowed through "phase-out provisions," which are triggered when your AGI reaches certain levels outlined in the current year income tax instructions. You can think of these as "phase-out levels." Thus your AGI has a big impact on your ultimate tax bill. In this sense, before AGI deductions have a larger impact on your ultimate tax liability because they lower your AGI.

The aforementioned phase-out levels typically increase every year or every couple of years to account for cost of living adjustments, so from year to year, there is not a tremendous difference in the phase-out levels. The common IRC after AGI deductions include:

- Mortgage interest on up to $1,000,000 in debt;
- Certain taxes, such as state and property tax;
- Medical and dental expenses in excess of 7.5% of AGI; and
- Charitable contributions.

Once you have determined your gross income and your AGI, you will want to tally up your after AGI deductions and compare them to the standard deduction to determine whether it is better to use after AGI deductions (also known as "itemizing") or to use the standard deduction. The standard deduction is in place to give tax payers relief if they do not have a certain dollar amount of after AGI deductions available for their tax return in a given year. In 2012, the standard deduction is $5,950 for singles and $11,900 for married filing jointly. Once you make this decision, you will then subtract personal and dependency exemptions of $3,800 each for you, your spouse, and children, to calculate your tax owed. The personal and dependency exemptions can be easily understood as a mechanism put in place to provide tax relief for all the daily costs of living that you and your loved ones face throughout the tax year. There are some expenses that are not deductible for our tax return, so it is nice to have the personal exemption, which indirectly covers some of our costs of living. Here is a hypothetical illustration of how a basic tax calculation works, assuming a single filer:

	Standard Deduction Scenario	Itemized Deduction Scenario
Gross Income	$100,000	$100,000
Before AGI Deductions	-$10,000	-$10,000
AGI	$90,000	$90,000
After AGI Deductions	-$5,950	-$7,000
Personal Exemptions	-$3,800	-$3,800
Taxable Income	$80,250	$79,200
Taxes Owed	$16,093	$15,830
Taxes Withheld	$16,000	$16,000
Refund (Payment Due)	($93)	$170

In the above scenario both singles have the same gross income and before AGI deductions. Where they differ is the after AGI deduction line. In the itemized deduction scenario, the individual was able to amass after AGI deductions greater than the dollar amount of the standard deduction of $5,950. As a result, the individual was able to take the greater of the two amounts on their tax return. In the hypothetical standard deduction scenario, we assume the person had only $4,000 of after AGI deductible expenses, and thus took the standard deduction, which was the higher amount. In this example, you can see how there is an advantage to being able to use itemized deductions rather than relying on the standard deduction.

Keep in mind that income taxes are important for our economy, so the deductions, though numerous, are not intended to allow us to deduct all of our personal expenses. It is important to keep in mind that we prepay our taxes during the year via payroll deductions. You are required to receive a W-2 each year, which will provide you the exact amount of taxes that were withheld during your tax year. This figure will reduce the taxes payable at the time of your tax filing, because you have already prepaid an amount shown on your W-2.

Further, there are various income tax credits available, which are based on AGI and generally only given in unique situations. Examples of credits include the earned income and child tax credits. Credits can change from year to year. Many of you probably remember the first-time homebuyer credit that was put in place to encourage home purchases during a downturn in the U.S. economy. These credits are generally put in place to encourage some type of behavior (such as home purchases) or to provide relief to those for which a tax liability would be overly burdensome. Tax credits are applied after you calculate taxable income and directly reduce your taxes owed.

Once you have considered your taxes withheld and any credits for which you are eligible, you will either owe a tax payment or get a refund. Many people of course are excited about their tax refund each year and can't wait to file their tax return. Others, who owe money, will wait until that dreaded day, usually the fifteenth day of the fourth month of the year, to make that tax payment. In my opinion, it is very important to ensure that your refund is not too significant. Before you throw me out as crazy, lean in and consider the following for a second. When you overpay your taxes through prepaid payroll deductions, you are in a sense giving the government an interest free loan, and worse, you lose the opportunity to use that money to make more money for yourself. At a minimum, you could put this money in a savings account that earns interest, rather than putting it in a government account for months, only to get that money (without interest) returned to you. This is a delicate balance. The government needs money for the entire year to operate, and to do so, it needs a steady stream of revenue in the form of our tax withholdings. The government wants to avoid the scenario wherein individuals do not withhold tax all year, only to pay a large lump sum in April. In fact, if you underpay your taxes by a certain amount, you will be assessed penalties by the IRS. If your withholdings are around 90% of your expected tax liability, you should avoid these type of penalties. Ideally, you should balance the requirement by the government to withhold taxes with your opportunity to use your earned income to pursue interest earnings or investment appreciation opportunities.

In summary:

1. Determine your gross income
2. Determine your before AGI deductions
3. Calculate AGI
4. Deduct after AGI or the standard deduction from AGI
5. Subtract your personal exemption
6. Calculate your taxes due using the IRS tax rate table
7. Compare to your taxes withheld on your W-2 to determine your additional payment or refund

AMTI: The Alternative Tax Universe

Just when you thought taxes were confusing enough (but hopefully less so after reading this chapter), the IRC provides us with an intriguing concept: alternative minimum taxable income ("AMTI") or alternative minimum tax ("AMT"), sometimes referred to as Form 6251. The intent of this regulation is to ensure that all people pay their fair share of taxes ("tentative minimum tax"). Form 6251 is another way to calculate your tax liability (akin to a parallel tax calculation) by forcing you to calculate a new taxable income (AMTI). The current AMTI rules use AMTI adjustments and preferences to transform traditional taxable income to AMTI. There is also an AMT exemption that decreases your AMTI. This is a calculation that must be performed annually. Later in this section I list the more common adjustments and preferences. Try not to get too overwhelmed with all the acronyms in this section. Just try to remember that alternative minimum tax is very similar to the tax principles you learned earlier in this section, with the exception of a few adjustments.

If you have dealt with AMTI in the past, you probably would have "preferred" to not deal with preferences and adjustments and anything else that raised your expected tax bill. Indeed, the AMTI rules can prove complex, confusing, and frustrating, given that taxes owed under AMTI rules can well exceed the taxes that would have been owed under the normal taxation calculation that was discussed earlier in this section. There is also some general disgruntlement that AMTI rules are causing the middle class to pay extra tax, when its initial intention was to curtail wealthy individuals from avoiding a fair tax liability.

You will not know your tax bill for the year until you run a tax calculation using the AMTI rules. A condensed AMTI formula is:

AMTI = Traditional Taxable income +/- AMT Adjustments + AMT Preferences

AMTI adjustments and preferences used in the above formula are mostly positive, which means that once you calculate what your taxable income is under standard tax rules, you add the following items to that amount to arrive at your AMTI (I included a few for illustrative purposes, but you can find a complete listing on Form 6251):

Adjustments (all positive) –

- Personal and dependency exemptions ($3,800 per person in 2012)
- Certain medical and dental deductions
- Certain state, local, and foreign income taxes deductible under normal tax rules
- Standard deduction (though you likely will itemize if you are under AMTI rules)
- Mortgage interest not related to acquiring, constructing, or substantially improving your house
- Miscellaneous deductions allowable under normal tax rules

Preferences (all positive) –

- Tax exempt interest on certain types of tax free bonds

In a sense, all you are doing is taking some of the deductions you took when calculating your regular tax, removing them, and then calculating a new taxable income. (Sounds fun, right?)

The next step in the process is to calculate a tentative minimum tax in the following manner:

Tentative Minimum Tax = (AMTI - AMT exemption) x AMT rate
(26% on first $175,000 of AMT taxable income and then 28% thereafter)

After performing this calculation, you can then compare it to your regular income tax. You may have noticed that the starting tax rate under AMT rules is 26% vs. 10% under the traditional tax rules. This ends up playing an important role in determining whether you will pay additional taxes. If tentative minimum tax is greater than your regular income tax, you will pay the tentative minimum tax. If tentative minimum tax is less than your regular income tax, you will pay your regular income tax.

Most high income earners who do not earn their income from some type of business will encounter AMT, especially in 2012 with the AMT exemption amount being reduced substantially from the prior year. In general, if the AMT exemption amount ($78,750 for married filing jointly or $50,600 for singles in 2012) exceeds the sum of your adjustments and preferences by a large margin, you should be okay from an AMT standpoint and not have to pay tax under AMT rules, (though this will not always be the case as AMT tax rates are higher on average than regular tax rates). The exemption amounts phase out as you start to earn more income, with the phase-out range beginning for AMTI circa $150,000 for married filing jointly (circa $112,000 for single filers). The key point of this AMT discussion is to raise awareness of AMT and what it can mean to our financial situation. If you earn above $100,000 as a single or $150,000 as married filing jointly, AMTI could be an issue for you. It is advisable to consult a CPA or CFP® professional as they will likely have experience with this issue and be able to develop certain tax planning strategies with you, based on your own unique situation.

Bringing it all together, below is a quick AMT calculation reference guide using hypothetical numbers:

Regular Taxable Income of $125,000

    +/- AMT Preferences and Adjustments of $25,000

    = AMTI of $150,000

        - AMT Exemption of $78,750

    = AMTI after Exemption - $71,250

    x AMT Tax Rate of 26%

    = Tentative Minimum Taxes Due of $18,525

     Taxes Due Under Regular Taxes of $23,310

    = Pay Higher Tax Amount of $23,310

In future years you could be eligible for a credit for the AMT you pay in a previous year, so keep that in mind if you are subject to AMT in the current year. You will need to file form 8801 to make that determination.

A natural question would then be, "how do I plan for AMT or minimize its effect?" It will depend on your personal facts and circumstances but one way would be to sit down and try to project your tentative minimum tax and regular tax in future years. If you notice that in the current year you will be subject to AMT, but are not projected to be impacted next year, you could delay a real estate purchase or certain medical expenses so that you will be able to take the interest, tax and expense deductions next year that would be added back for AMT purposes in the current year.

A word of caution: the above was simplified for illustrative purposes. Generally the AMT exemption will phase out and usually the AMT tax rate will be a blend of 26% and 28% rates. On the IRS website, there is a tool that is designed to help you determine whether you will be subject to additional tax liability under AMT rules. It is certainly worth looking at if you are planning on attempting this calculation yourself. Please consult a tax professional if you are having trouble calculating an additional tax liability under the alternative minimum tax rules.

How to Lower the Amount of Income Taxes You Pay

You just learned the basics of how the income tax calculation works, so now it may be helpful to do a deeper dive into what can be done to lower the amount of income taxes paid. As illustrated previously, a key starting point for tax planning is determining whether you are going to take the standard deduction or be eligible to take the itemized deduction. These are both after AGI deductions. The determining factor in whether you are going to use a standard or itemized deduction lies in the amount of expenses you have during the year and the type of expenditures. If you are making more than $100,000 a year and not able to use the standard deduction, it is probably because you A) rent and/or B) do not give enough money to charity.

In the United States, we have a graduated tax system. What this means is that a portion of your income will be taxed at 10%, some at 15% and then the remaining income at 25% and higher. Using the Form 1040 tax table in your tax instructions, it becomes clear that there is a need for tax planning. You can quickly see how your income falls into various tax percentage bands. The tax rate range for US Federal Income tax is 10% - 35%. Below is a 2012 version of the Form 1040 Schedule X that I modified slightly to make it easier to understand. This schedule provides a nice summary for a single individual filing a tax return (use the schedule Y-1 table if married filing jointly):

If Taxable Income Is Over:	But Not Over:	Tax Bracket You Fall In	Tax You Pay
$0	$8,700	10%	$8,700 X 10%
$8,700	$35,350	15%	$870 + (($35,350 – $8,700) X 15%)
$35,350	$85,650	25%	$4,867.5 + (($85,650 – $35,350) X 25%)
$85,650	$178,650	28%	$17,442.5 + (($178,650 – $85,650) X 28%)
$178,650	$388,350	33%	$43,482.5 + (($388,350 – $178,650) X 33%)
$388,350	----------	35%	$112,683.5 + ((Income – $388,350) X 35%)

As you can see, the ability to deduct more expenses (and thus lower your taxable income) using the itemized deduction becomes a powerful concept, given the small margin between the 10% tax bracket and the 25% tax bracket. As this book was going to print, the tax tables for 2013 were released. The most substantive change was the introduction of a top tax rate of 39.6% for taxable income over $400,000 (over $450,000 for married filing jointly). The introduction of the 39.6% tax rate made the 35% tax bracket smaller. All other tax brackets were adjusted for inflation. The following sections discuss common ways to lower your income taxes.

Mortgage Interest Can Lower Your Tax Bill

A common large itemized deduction is mortgage interest. Our country's tax system encourages ownership of a house through the ability to deduct qualified mortgage interest. The standard deduction is large enough that typically you will not see a significant difference between the itemized and standard deduction if you do not have deductible mortgage interest. As stated previously, the goal is for us to lower our taxable income number. A house can give you the double win benefit of providing a place to live, while also allowing you to deduct mortgage interest and the related real estate property tax. You can then use the itemized deduction (mortgage interest alone can be close to or equal to the standard deduction). This does not mean that you should buy a house to get a tax deduction. Buying a house is a very serious decision and the available tax deduction should be low on your priority list in comparison to things like location, safety, re-sale potential, and length of time you expect to live in the house. To see how the tax benefit works, consider the following scenario:

Person A has a blended 25% tax rate and makes a $1,000 per month mortgage payment. (Assume for simplicity that it is an interest only loan and that this particular payment is all interest).

Person B has a blended 25% tax rate and pays $1,000 per month for rent.

	Renter	Homeowner
Housing Payment	$1,000	$1,000
Tax Benefit	$0	$250
Net Cost of Payment	$1,000	$750

In this scenario, Person A will have a $250 tax benefit and Person B will not. This is because Person A will be able to lower taxable income by $1,000 using an itemized deduction, and his or her $1,000 will not be taxed at 25%. This is a pretty powerful concept because in each scenario, Person A and Person B pay the same amount of money, but have two different tax consequences. In addition to the tax benefit, if housing prices are going up (not necessarily a safe assumption given real estate in the past few years), Person A will have an equity position in their house, whereas Person B will make a rent payment and get no further benefit beyond having a roof over their head.

A Word of Caution: Don't Let the Tax Tail Wag the Dog

While I was studying for my accounting degree, tax class would get interesting sometimes, (yep, only sometimes), when an adventurous student would try to stump our tax professor, Connie Kuertz, with unrealistic tax scenarios that made little economic sense, with the only aim being a potential tax deduction. Time and time again, Professor Kuertz's response would be, "Don't let the tax tail wag the dog." In other words, don't do something because the primary motivation is to get a tax deduction, especially if it doesn't make economic sense. This point cannot be over emphasized. I have seen people get into second houses or start businesses for tax reasons, but they lose sight of the number one goal of any financial endeavor, which is to make a profit. A house of course is no different. If we learn anything from the past, it should be that buying a house is a very important decision and not one to be done primarily for the tax benefit. I view the tax benefit and the deductible mortgage interest as excellent by-products of owning a house, but they will never be my primary motivation for owning a house. If owning a house would put me in an economically challenging loan or in a house that will not be easy to resell in the future, I would much rather rent until the right house appears. This is where short-term vs. long-term thinking comes into play. Paying a little more tax in a year where you feel compelled to rent because there are no good housing options is much better than settling for a house, paying slightly less in tax, but then being stuck with a house that you cannot easily pay for now or sell in the future.

During the housing bubble of the mid 2000's, it seemed like everyone wanted to get in the "buy a property and flip it" game. The idea was that you could get a loan, make little or no down payment, fix up the house or wait for the market to jump, and then sell it for a profit. When property values are moving upward, this strategy can pay off handsomely. The use of debt (which is sometimes referred to as "leverage") to finance an investment, can exacerbate both returns and losses on that investment. Unfortunately, when the market declined significantly, plenty of people were left with investment property that was no longer worth the initial purchase price. As a result, they owed more money than the property was worth ("negative equity"), and because many of these owners had put very little of their own money into their property, they did not have a tremendous economic incentive to stick with the property and make the mortgage payments. Some irresponsible property owners viewed this as a reason to stop paying their mortgage, leaving banks or securitization vehicles with loans that would not be repaid, (banks or investors then had to take millions of dollars of losses on loans), and a large inventory of foreclosed properties. Others did not miss payments intentionally, but were stretched so thin by having too much debt and not enough income, and thus had no choice but to foreclose on their property.

The first thought that came to me when I learned of this occurrence was, "How unfair! There should be some way to penalize these people for their actions." I learned later that there is such a mechanism. In most states, the lender will take some type of judicial action toward the borrower, which could include the use of liens on other individual asset holdings or some type of wage garnishment. This is broadly called recourse. It is definitely something to consider when contemplating whether or not to foreclose on a house. In today's environment, loan servicers are much more willing to work with borrowers to come up with a payment plan or reduction of the loan than they were in the past. I gather that when real estate markets were good, the use of recourse was rare because a loan servicer generally would not have a tremendous issue obtaining a house for $280,000 that has a $180,000 loan on it. The loan servicer could sell for a gain and close the loan. Furthermore, individuals that have equity in a house through their own payments and market appreciation are less likely to walk away from a house. Generally, I have found that in today's housing market, a loan servicer would rather modify a loan than seize a house from a borrower and sell it for below market value. Further judicial action can be both costly and time consuming, so it is beneficial for both the loan servicer and the borrower to come to an amicable solution.

It has been theorized that from a pure financial perspective, a mortgage payment is akin to a "call option" on the house. A call option is the right (but not obligation) to buy an asset at a certain price. If you are familiar with this term, it is usually used in connection with stock. Stock options are a common type of executive compensation. You can also buy call options on a variety of stocks. I will discuss call options later in this book. In relation to real estate, as long as property values are going up, property owners are happy with exercising their "call option" because every payment they make gives them a greater ownership percentage in a house that is going to be worth more in the future. It's similar to if you have a call option on a stock at a price of $50 when the stock is selling for $53. You would absolutely pay $50 for a $53 stock, and home owners, for example, would be willing to make a monthly payment on a $180,000 mortgage for a property that is worth $200,000. However, think for a moment about the other scenario. Would you pay $50 for a stock that was currently selling on the open market for $45? Of course not! You would pay $45 and let your call option expire, unexercised. Many speculative real estate investors were faced with an analogous situation. Predictably, with the recent economic downturn, investors decided it was not worth making their monthly payment on their $180,000 mortgage when the asset (or house) tied to that mortgage was only worth $120,000.

This is where ethics and financial intelligence can be in conflict. At one time I owned a house that was worth much less than the mortgage. You have probably heard that this is called "underwater." As in real life, being underwater on a house for a long period of time can be a helpless situation with grave financial consequences. When in situations of dire need, we humans tend to rationalize anything in hopes of survival. Clearly, being underwater on a mortgage is not a matter of life or death, but financial difficulties can cause unimaginable stress. I remember struggling with the decision to keep making payments on my underwater house. I first tried to refinance, (something I would advise exploring if your current debt terms are less than ideal), but the appraisal on my house had fallen so far below the balance owed on my loan, that it was not approved. All my financial training taught me that it didn't make sense to keep paying this crippling loan. However, my heart kept interceding and told me that it was right for me to honor my obligation to pay my mortgage, no matter the price. How could I write a book to you all about financial freedom and responsibility if I was walking away from my obligations freely, causing the bank that loaned me the money to suffer (or investment vehicle invested in the loan to suffer)? You may be thinking, "Who cares about the bank? They have plenty of money." If everyone decided to abandon their property and stop paying their mortgage, you can imagine that this would actually have a devastating effect on loan originators, securitization vehicles, the related investors, and the overall economy. I believe we all impact the state of our economy, and I am absolutely certain that if we all were a bit more responsible with our finances, we could change the entire trajectory of our economy and change the trajectory of our financial future in the process.

Rather than preoccupying yourself with housing deductions or becoming the next real estate millionaire, buy a house because you like the house and can see yourself living in that area for a long time. Though we can never entirely predict the future, buying a house because you want to itemize on your tax return can have negative financial consequences if you later try to sell the house and struggle to find buyers. The real estate market some of us grew up in has changed, and though I want to believe that we will see housing prices go up again to previous levels, there is a real problem right now with excess housing inventory and homeowners with negative equity. It is important to enjoy the tax benefit of deducting interest on your mortgage, but don't do it at the expense of being captive to a home or having to sell it under distressed conditions. If you aren't sure where you want to live, or if you consider your current geography to be a short-term arrangement, renting can be a smart decision. Don't let a tax deduction be the primary driver for your housing decision. Don't let the tax tail wag the dog.

How Giving Really Gives Back

Giving to others truly pays off on your tax return. The US tax system's generous tax deductions offered for qualified charitable contributions makes giving worthwhile for financial planning purposes. Qualified charitable contributions can be as simple as the money you are asked to donate to a local cause every time you make a purchase at the grocery store, to giving to your local Church, to giving to local relief efforts. When donating a gift, it is important to ensure that the IRS recognizes that organization as a qualified charitable organization for tax return purposes. Section 501(c)(3) of the IRC gives guidance regarding what constitutes a charitable organization. There is an upper limit on the deductibility of charitable contributions made in a given year. All of your cash contributions to qualified charities will be tax deductible up to either 30% or 50% of your AGI. If you decide to donate items other than cash, such as a stock or property, the deduction limits change to 30% of AGI for 50% of AGI charities and 20% of AGI for 30% of AGI charities. The most common 50% of AGI organizations are churches, educational institutions, and hospitals, but there are other organizations that meet the criteria. A 30% of AGI charity is simply one that does not qualify as a 50% of AGI charity, which, according to IRS guidance (Publication 526), could include a fraternity or veteran's organization.

For example, if your AGI in a given year is $10, then you are eligible for up to $5 in charitable deductions if you contribute cash to a 50% AGI charity. You could also take up to a $3 charitable deduction if you donated $3 in stock to this same organization, in lieu of making the cash donation. Before contributing to an organization, it is advisable to ask them to provide evidence that the IRS recognizes them as a 501(c)(3) charity. Assuming the same $10 AGI as above, if you are contributing to a 30% of AGI organization, your deductible cash contribution will be limited to $3 (or $2 if you are gifting stock).

The charitable contribution limits are, in my opinion, quite high, and it would be difficult for the majority of us to give away 30% to 50% of our AGI in cash donations. I discern that this is done on purpose so that people have a great tax incentive to donate to charities. Further, if for some reason you contribute more than 50% of your AGI, you are able to "carry over" that charitable contribution to be deducted on a future return when your charitable contributions are less than 50% of AGI. You are able to carry over the charitable contribution disallowed in a current year to your next five tax returns. If you are not able to use up all of your disallowed contribution over the next five tax returns, then you lose the portion that was disqualified. I find it unlikely that most of us will end up with disallowed charitable contributions, so the key point in all of this is that you should feel confident that, under normal circumstances, your charitable contributions will eventually be tax deductible.

If you are dealing with an organization that is unwilling to demonstrate their filing status to the IRS, it may be safer to donate your money to a different organization that is willing to prove that they are recognized by the IRS as a qualified charitable organization. If you donate to a new charity that is in the process of getting a qualified status, your contributions can be deductible once that charity gets approval from the IRS. For example, if you make a donation in the current year, but the IRS doesn't approve the organization's application until the following year, you can list this donation as a deduction on your tax return in the following year.

Understanding How Real Estate Activities Can Reduce Your Taxes

Before the recent U.S. real estate market crash, it was not uncommon to hear of people burning the candle at both ends, working their normal occupation or business during the day and then pursuing a real estate business on the side. Infomercials were rampant, proclaiming that people were making thousands a month in real estate. How could we refuse that sweet deal? It is important to understand that running a real estate business on the side is not a guaranteed money maker, nor the golden grail of tax shelters. As it is with a lot of things in life, if an idea is too good to be true, it probably is. The IRS is very in tune with the potential for real estate ownership to be used as an opportunity to wash out taxable income and as such, has provided some strict criteria for what real estate expenses are deductible and when one would qualify at all to receive real estate expense deductions (aside from deductible mortgage interest). The IRC has built in tax deduction relief for individuals and entities that rely on real estate as their livelihood, but these same benefits do not extend to individuals that have a real estate venture as a hobby. The burden of proof is on the tax return preparer to demonstrate why they have determined that real estate expenses are tax deductible. It is important not to be overly zealous when pursuing real estate deductions. Before considering a real estate venture and the treatment on your tax return, it is beneficial to understand some important guidelines.

The IRC has a special term it uses for activities that they do not view the same way as a typical business venture: "passive activity." This distinction is important because if your venture is considered an active business, there is an ability to deduct legitimate business expenses on your tax return. However, if your activity is considered passive, your ability to deduct expenses related to this venture are limited. The IRC specifically cites rental activity as a type of passive activity, which means that you cannot buy a property, rent it out, and then start deducting all the related expenses of up-keep on your tax return. One way for your real estate venture to not be considered a passive activity is if the IRS does not consider your property to be a rental property. The tax code has six conditions and if you meet one of them, your real estate venture is not considered a rental. The specifics are located in the IRC and can be found by doing a quick internet search. These six exceptions are typically not going to be met by someone who has a second home that they are renting out to college kids. If you are somehow successful in meeting one of these exceptions, you still must prove you are a material participant in that real estate venture, which is usually dependent on the number of hours you contribute to the endeavor. If you do not, your activity will still be considered passive, and you will only be able to deduct losses or expenses on your rental against other passive income you gain (which could be zero if you are just holding a real estate property in hopes of price appreciation, in which case you would not deduct anything).

There is an exception to these rules if you are a real estate professional, as it is assumed that real estate is an active business and not a passive activity for real estate professionals. You can also partially deduct losses on your real estate investments if you can prove that you actively participated in the rental of it and that you have a material ownership in the property. However, deductions become disallowed once you reach a certain AGI. For instance, if your AGI on your most recent tax return is $200,000, you will not be able to deduct any of your losses on your rental property against your active income, with active income mostly being the salary you earned during the year. The most important thing you can do is check the tax rules carefully before starting a business venture where you do not expect to be a material participant or a business venture that involves real estate. Moving forward without understanding the tax implications could be a costly move.

This could be an eye opener to some, and hopefully it makes it clear that the burden is on the individual to demonstrate that he or she is in the real estate business (rather than just having a property that is rented out in a passive manner). Most people aren't trying to become a licensed real estate agent when they decide to buy a house to rent out and eventually sell for a gain. This section provided a good general understanding of the considerations that should be made and the "tests" that need to be done to see how to treat real estate expenses on your tax return. If you feel like your own situation is "grey" or you need further guidance, it is worthwhile to reach out to a licensed tax professional for additional guidance. This individual should be able to point you to a reasonable conclusion, give you confidence in that conclusion, and support you in the chance that the IRS has a question about the treatment of your business or real estate related expenses.

To Rent or Buy?

Before moving off the topic of real estate, it is important to discuss whether you should rent or buy a house. Remember the earlier discussion about the "tax tail wagging the dog?" I remember being a new graduate in 2005 and looking for a place to live in Atlanta. I did not even consider the option of renting (oops). As a soon to be Certified Public Accountant, I remember thinking back to my tax training and itemized deductions. A predominant thought of mine was that I needed the tax deduction of owning a house and also wanted to add equity to my own personal balance sheet. Did I worry about a mortgage and the possibility of owing more on my house than what I could sell it for in the future? Of course not! Real estate only goes up in value, right? I never thought about the possibility of real estate going down! If I was lucky, I thought, I could make enough money to hold that property, rent it out, and live happily ever after. Of course 2008 came and my one bedroom condo wasn't worth as much as I originally agreed to pay for it. I had a great tax deduction, was living in a place I loved, but I was losing money daily on the property. I learned the hard way, but you can learn the easy way by learning from my mistake. So many people go through life learning from their own mistakes. Trial and error is good for a science project, but not as effective in the game of life, when you can learn from the mistakes of others and not endure the pains of "error." Some call this true wisdom, and I agree. Regarding real estate investments, it could be beneficial to pay heed to the following three rules:

- **Only buy a residence if you envision yourself there for the long-term.** Real estate is more appropriately classified as a long-term investment. For a lot of people in the United States, a house is the largest asset on the family balance sheet (but remember, a lot of times it has a big debt balance attached to it). The house is unique in that it serves a basic human need to have a dwelling, but it is also a long-term asset that can improve your family's wealth through its potential price appreciation. The IRC provides an exciting benefit to individuals and couples, wherein any gain on a primary residence resided in for greater than two years is excluded from tax (up to $250,000 for single and $500,000 for married filing jointly). Buying a house without a long-term view could put you in a situation where you can't afford to sell the house yet due to current market prices. If you are unsure about what to do, renting is a very safe option that will give you the flexibility to take advantage of a great housing opportunity when you have the ability or the desire to make a long-term commitment to a residence.

- **Before purchasing a residence, do some research on the long-term outlook of the community.** As stated before, this is a long-term investment, and thus all factors that will impact the ability for this asset to return value should be considered. It is generally advisable to avoid being among the first group of people to move into a community. A neighborhood with a lot of unsold houses is a bit of a warning sign and should be something that prompts us to ask a lot of questions. For example, moving into a relatively vacant community that has Home Owners Association ("HOA") dues can bring with it tremendous hidden or unpredictable expenses, as you may find yourself paying more than your fair share of community expenses if the community does not have enough home owners to spread out the HOA operating costs. Another concern is moving into any area with obvious excess supply. This is more likely to occur with condos, which can be built high rise style and in concentrated spaces. The last thing you want is to buy in an area that gets overbuilt, as it will likely impact your selling price later, jeopardizing the possibility of you earning a long-term gain on your residence.

- **Do research on the school district associated with your house.** This should be more thorough than just relying on your realtor saying, "This is a great school district." Look into school testing scores, crime occurrences within the perimeter of the school, and the school facilities. If you have kids, moving into a great public school district can save thousands of dollars that would otherwise be allocated toward private schooling. The ability to take this money saved and allocate it toward funding college or retirement will have an enormous impact on family wealth. Further, even if you don't have kids or plan on having kids, the person buying your house may have kids or plan on having kids, and a good school district could be the difference between them buying the house or walking away from the buying table.

If I could do it all over again, I would have rented after college. I think I made the mistake of seeing only the appreciation side of real estate, rather than being thorough and deliberate in my decision making. I am glad you are reading this book because it could help you discover something in your search that will help you to avoid making the same mistake I did. As a renter, you lose the tax benefit, but you gain more dwelling flexibility. I think of losing the tax deduction of renting as indirectly being an option that you purchase for the flexibility to move quickly (rather than having to go through the process of trying to list and sell a home). Once you buy a house, you exchange your housing flexibility option for a mortgage and the hope that your house will be marketable in the future and produce a long-term gain. Be deliberate in your search, and you will increase your chances of making the right decision as it relates to real estate. Avoid getting caught up in the emotion that goes along with making a housing purchase.

Is it a Business or a Hobby?

In this section, there is some overlap with the previous section on real estate, but I felt it was important to cover all types of businesses (not just real estate) and the potential implications from a tax perspective. As alluded to earlier, our tax code is very focused on preventing individuals from running a side business that is really just for fun, is losing a lot of money, and in the end becomes nothing more than a way to deduct "fun expenses" on a tax return. A perfect example is baseball card collecting (remember when people actually did that!). For most people that have done this in their lifetime, it was considered a hobby. One could buy, sell and trade baseball cards, and incur numerous expenses in the process. If one got involved enough, it would be easy to say, "I am in the business of buying and selling baseball cards." It would certainly not to be unlikely to imagine a situation where one is an office worker by day and a baseball card collector by night. If someone has the discipline and energy to succeed at both endeavors, it is admirable, but is the latter activity actually a business for tax purposes? The answer lies in proving to the IRS that this baseball card collecting activity is not just an extracurricular activity that is incurring expenses for tax reduction purposes.

Simply stated, your side business needs to be legitimate and actually earn money once every three years. Intuitively, a business is usually started with the end goal of breaking a profit. If after three years, your baseball card collecting business is just you buying baseball cards and sitting on a huge inventory of baseball cards, how is it different than not having a baseball card business and buying cards to put in your closet? It is not uncommon for an individual to have a day job and run a business in their free time, especially during the initial stages of the business. The business needs cash flow, and sometimes a stable job can provide the initial supporting cash flow for an independent business. Just make sure to operate your business like it is a business. Things like keeping a separate bank account for the business, having a company mission statement, and possessing company letterhead or business cards can go a long way in proving the legitimacy of the business with others and the IRS. Also, it is imperative that you file tax returns for your business. The IRS provides the following guidance when trying to determine whether a venture is a hobby or a business:

- Does the time and effort put into the activity indicate an intention to make a profit?
- Does the taxpayer depend on income from the activity?
- If there are losses, are they due to circumstances beyond the taxpayer's control or did they occur in the start-up phase of the business?
- Has the taxpayer changed methods of operation to improve profitability?
- Does the taxpayer or his/her advisors have the knowledge

needed to carry on the activity as a successful business?
- Has the taxpayer made a profit in similar activities in the past?
- Does the activity make a profit in some years?
- Can the taxpayer expect to make a profit in the future from the appreciation of assets used in the activity?

The IRS guidance then goes on to give a presumption that a differentiating factor between whether a venture is a business or hobby can depend on whether there has been a profit during three of the past five tax years. This is not an automatic requirement, and certain special cases can be made for why a business would not yet be profitable three out of five years. If your activity is deemed a hobby rather than a business, the deductibility of expenses is vastly different. When recognized as a business, the expenses can likely be deducted before AGI. If the venture is deemed to be a hobby, qualifying expenses can be deducted after AGI, as itemized deductions. Not all expenses will qualify, but as hobby related expenses are limited in scope, ensure you get help from a CPA or other tax professional if you are unsure about whether a certain expense will qualify for a tax deduction.

One other point on the subject of starting a business: the legal structure of the business you select is of vital importance. There is a difference in the tax accounting between starting up a sole proprietorship versus an S-Corporation versus a Limited Liability Corporation ("LLC"). Choosing the wrong formation can lead to paying the wrong amount in taxes, filling out more tax forms than necessary, or making it more difficult to get additional capital if you are interested in expanding your operations. There is also the employer side of payroll taxes (Social Security and Medicare) that will need to be accounted for depending on the form of business you choose. Consult legal literature on the advantages and disadvantages of each business form before you start your own company. Personally, I think it is advantageous to avoid the sole proprietorship business model if possible, because as a sole proprietorship, the lone business owner is subject to strict liability for the actions of the business. This means that creditors of your business can come after your personal assets (such as your home) if the business fails to meet its obligations. Furthermore, you may end up paying more in tax under this business form. As always, facts and circumstances will dictate the best business form for your company.

Save your receipts. Documentation retention is very important when trying to support the legitimacy of your business and any related tax deductions you attempt to take on your tax return. On the occasion that the IRS has a question about your return, it will be of vital importance to be able to quickly provide documentation to support your tax position. It could make sense to invest in an inexpensive file that you can use for each year's tax returns and supporting documentation. You can also "go green" and develop a good retention system on your computer. The last thing you want is to get a question from the IRS about a deduction you are taking and have to scramble for supporting documentation, only to find out the documentation is missing or is not readily available. When the IRS asks questions about a return, they are expecting a timely response, so there will not be a lot of time to reconstruct a lot of the supporting documentation that was used when you filled out your prior year tax return. In most cases, the IRS can ask questions about a tax return for three years from the date you filed that tax return (certain exceptions apply, such as if there is fraud or a large underpayment in tax). Can you imagine trying to go find a receipt from four years ago? Spare yourself the anxiety of trying to re-piece a past return and develop a sound organizational system of saving physical receipts with a file system or saving receipts electronically on your computer. If you hire a CPA to do your tax return, they should be well acquainted with documentation retention policies and thus should be able to alleviate your concerns of thinking about past tax returns.

Hiring Help

This of course begs the question, "Should I hire tax help or not?" As a CPA and CFP® professional, this would be my place to promote the use of hired certified professionals (but I saved an entire chapter for that ☺). Whether to hire a certified professional to help with your taxes is going to depend on your specific facts and circumstances. Online tax software has gotten very good, and for an individual with a very simple tax situation, paying the money to use this software can be the smart play. The online software does a good job of taking you step by step through your return and is well versed in anticipating the more general deductions that are available to save you money. Once an individual starts getting into complex investing, has a stake in a partnership, earns income in multiple states, or has a personal business, hiring help can be very beneficial and is highly recommended. In general, the more income you earn and the more stuff you buy or do, the more important it will be to have effective tax planning. Hiring a tax professional for $500 so you can save $1000 is a no brainer. This tangible benefit does not even account for the intangible benefit of being released from the stress of managing a complex tax situation or worrying about what would happen if the IRS decided to audit your tax return.

Also keep in mind that online software doesn't provide you with true customized tax planning, which is where you generally will save the most money on taxes. Additionally, hiring an expert helps take out some of the uncertainty of whether the tax position you took on your return would stand up if challenged by the IRS. Also in some situations the hired help will support you in an IRS audit. It is also not a bad idea to hire a tax lawyer if you have an incredibly complex tax situation. Lastly, it is a time saver to have a hired certified professional handle the administrative burden of filing and preparing tax returns. If you have a very busy schedule (and who doesn't), hiring a certified professional to manage your tax situation can be well worth the money, in administrative relief alone.

Conclusion

As you can see after reading this chapter, the key to excelling in the area of taxes is preparation, which again is where tax software is lacking. Plan early and plan often. You can do this preparation on your own, partner with a certified professional, or put it entirely in the hands of a certified professional. At the start of every year before you do your New Year's Resolutions, you should think about your tax plan. I know it is much more fun to think about losing 15 pounds than saving $15 dollars on your tax return, but being deliberate in your approach to taxes can be very beneficial. Tax is an area a lot of us dread and wait until the last minute to think about, sometimes a few weeks before our tax filing is due. The problem with this strategy is that at that point there is not much you can do about your taxes. For individuals, a tax return is on a twelve month basis and the reporting period effectively ends on December 31st. Why do we spend so little time on an area that has such a big impact on our financial futures? So, next year when you make your New Year's resolution to lose 15 pounds, bring a notebook (or electronic tablet) to the gym, and jot down your tax plan while tearing it up on the treadmill. You will be so glad you did it!

I think we would all be better off financially if we drew up an annual plan for ourselves, so that at the onset of the year we could have a better idea of what type of income and expenses we expected. Corporations do this all the time, and it's called budgeting. Typically, most corporations have a financial planning and analysis group that spends a lot of time thinking about the revenue and expense outlook for the year and revisiting it at various times of the year to ensure the company is on track or determine whether an outlook needs to be modified. We are all capable of doing something similar. If we are expecting a lot of expenses in one year, maybe we need to decrease our 401(k) contributions to guarantee we have enough cash on hand to meet these obligations without resorting to credit cards or other forms of borrowing. If we are expecting a big bonus one year, maybe we want to consider deferring some of that income or putting more in our 401(k) account to avoid AMT, and thus save ourselves from paying more in taxes. In summary, having a plan puts us in a better position to win financially in the area of taxes than we would without a tax plan. It would be discouraging to pay more in taxes at the end of year just because we failed to adequately prepare for our annual tax obligation.

Investments Principles

I like to watch sports, and when I do, sometimes I see those commercials with little babies managing their online investment trading account. The message is subtle, but powerful: investing can be so easy, even a little kid can do it. I think this message is only partially correct. I believe anyone can make an investment, provided they have adequate capital, but not everyone can consistently make desirable returns on those investments. It is just not that easy. Other commercials would agree, and are anxious to tell you about the quality of their investment products and professionals. But how do you know that these companies do not have massive conflicts of interest, defaulting to selling their own products even if more desirable investments are knowingly available? How do you know that these mutual funds are really beating the market average after accounting for the fees they charge? The intent may not even be deceitful, but perhaps the investment professional really only knows their own products. What if the investment professional advising you on investment decisions has not made a pledge to abide by a strict code of ethics?

If we learned anything from the past few years it is this: investing is so much more than following a colored line. There is uncertainty, there is risk, and there is diligence required. I think that is probably why some of the investments commercials appeal to us. We want a sense of comfort when investing, a feeling that there are people out there that have this perfectly under control and can help us so we don't lose money, no matter the state of the economy. Ultimately, we want to feel like we can trust the person that is advising us on our investments, and once we build that trust, we want to feel like these professionals will help us reach our investment goals.

We all have dreams and desires; we also know that it is going to take money to fund these objectives. A money making vehicle other than our own direct labor is usually required to meet these objectives. Investments are a logical choice, because you can plow money into them and primarily the only decision remaining is how long to hold the investment before you sell it. It sounds very straight forward, but do not let the simplicity in form make it sound like it is simplicity in substance.

There are many goals for this section of the book. Primarily, I would like to dispel some of the common myths about investing, equip you with an investment vocabulary, help you understand the seriousness of setting up your "asset mix" (and the related rebalancing), and lastly, motivate you to get more involved in this area of your finances. These goals will be baked into terms and concepts that may be familiar to you. For many, when investments are discussed, 401(k) plans or an equivalent defined contribution plan comes to mind. As such, the beginning of this discussion will be about investments in the context of a 401(k). The remainder of the chapter will focus on other investment fundamentals that could prove helpful as you become more comfortable with investments and their role in your wealth creation process.

Introduction to the 401(k) Plan

The period of 2001-2006 showed excellent equity growth that had many people excited about their 401(k) portfolios and sold on the idea of pumping any available cash into their 401(k) account. I could hear people for miles saying, "you don't invest in a 401(k)? You must be crazy!" And given the strong returns over the period (e.g. the S&P 500 grew by approximately 7.5% over the period), this mindset was understandable. For those that have heard the term, but aren't exactly sure, 401(k) is code name for a defined contribution plan offered to employees by a sponsored employer. (The name 401(k) comes from the IRC, where this type of plan is discussed.) Generally, the employer incents its employees to contribute to a 401(k) plan by offering to match a percentage of employee contributions up to a certain amount. In addition, pre-tax contributions are limited by the IRC (up to $17,500 in 2013; $17,000 in 2012). A common matching convention would be that an employer matches 50% of all contributions up to 6% of total contributions. A common myth about the 401(k) is that it is a necessity to contribute solely because there is "free money" in the match.

If I go to the casino tomorrow and bet $100 because my employer will match $6 of it, would that be a sound decision?

This is an exaggeration, but it is trying to illustrate that you should not base an investing decision primarily on the premise that if you make the investment, you will have someone else put in more on your behalf. If I could tell you tomorrow that a stock was going from $100 to $0 and that I will match 100% of your contributions, would this be intriguing to you? I'd say you would probably decline that deal, despite the large match. This doesn't mean that the match isn't a great benefit, it just shouldn't be the sole reason why you invest in a 401(k) plan. As I will explain later, your decision about whether to invest and what to invest in should be a function of your risk preferences and return requirements. In essence I want you to think more strategically about your 401(k) plan, and get beyond the match and the "long-term returns" of equity markets. The strength of equity markets in the long-run is proven over certain sample periods; the long-term return on equity markets may not necessarily be the same return you get on your 401(k) investments. Like most things in life, there are advantages and disadvantages to a 401(k) plan that should be objectively considered. I am not attempting to persuade or dissuade you, but rather to inform you. My hope is that the following discussion will give you an opportunity to make an objective decision.

What if my Employer Does Not Have a 401(K) plan?

Also, before I dive deeper into the 401(k) investment model, if your company does not have a 401(k) plan or does not provide you with some other type of retirement plan at work, it is advisable to consider a traditional IRA. As mentioned in the tax section, contributions to a traditional IRA are before AGI deductions (up to $5,000 or $6,000 if you are age 50 or older) and achieve a similar goal as a 401(k) plan in providing a tax efficient way to save for retirement.

You can invest in a traditional IRA if you are covered by an employee sponsored retirement plan; however, you may only be able to take a partial or no tax deduction depending on your income levels. Per the IRC, in 2012 married filing jointly taxpayers could take the full $5,000 IRA deduction if their modified AGI was $92,000 or less. The deduction started to phase out between greater than $92,000 and less than $112,000 in 2012, with no deduction allowed at all for couples with modified AGI at $112,000 or more. In 2013 the IRA contribution limits were bumped up an extra $500.

401(k) Disadvantages

1. Returns Are Not Guaranteed

401(k) investments are not guaranteed in their performance and, depending on the time period of investment, may not have a return that is in line with historical returns on the S&P 500 (a common US investing benchmark). Your 401(k) mutual fund investments may not even beat the market return in a given year after accounting for mutual fund expenses. We are in an environment now where we have seen the governments of strong countries get downgraded or face the threat of a downgrade. Historically, many of us have considered government debt issued by countries with strong economies to be safe, (and even so safe that it feels like it is guaranteed). If a rating agency is concerned to the point where it would downgrade debt issued by established nations, what does that say about our investment in a 401(k), which can include a wide array of "riskier" investments? How often is it that 401(k) investors are placing some of their money in "safe" fixed income investments and some in "U.S. equity" investments, and if they are really adventurous, putting some money in a "foreign" investment fund? The mix could be equally distributed, heavy towards fixed income, or heavy towards equity. However, I wonder if sometimes we are just doing this blindly, and hoping that in the end all of the investments will go up in value to some degree, and we will be better off as a result. Maybe some of us revisit our allocation every few years or annually. The reality is that the mutual funds you select through a 401(k) plan are not guaranteed and are limited in their depth and breadth. Just because an expert is managing the fund you invest in, does not guarantee that you will earn a positive return or exceed a comparable benchmark return.

2. 401(k) Plans Have Fees and Are Managed By Fund Managers… Who Aren't Always Perfect

The funds that we are putting our money in have managers that run them; there are fees to consider that haircut our potential returns. In addition, not all fund managers are created equal. Fund managers have bad performance years and fund families may underperform the market during the period of time that you are most concerned about growing your portfolio. It is not uncommon for an active investment manager to underperform a common index, such as the S&P 500 (a common benchmark for US equity investors). Mutual funds can underperform for a number of reasons, but one of the big contributors to underperformance are the fees that investors pay for the operation and management of the fund. For example, if a fund manager were to copy the S&P 500 exactly, that fund would still underperform the benchmark, because investors would need to pay expenses that impact the return of the fund, but not the S&P 500.

There are a few things you can look at to evaluate fund managers prior to investing in your 401(k). You can compare a fund to other funds with similar strategies to see how the fund you are thinking of pursuing compares to the median or middle performing fund. I would not use this is as an absolute benchmark for performance, but instead I would use it as a way to compare other fund managers in the absence of more specific information. Imagine a scenario where you are investing in a certain U.S. equity mutual fund as part of your 401(k) investment portfolio, and that fund is producing an annual return that is worse than published returns on similar funds. At that point it may be time to reevaluate whether you should continue to withhold money from your paycheck and invest in the underperforming fund. This seems very obvious, but it does take some extra work on your part to make sure your investment returns are competitive with similar products in the available fund universe.

The concern is that many people blindly invest in their 401(k) without doing a hard evaluation of its performance or whether the money could be better invested elsewhere. You cannot depend on your employers to always provide you with the best available investment opportunities as part of our 401(k) program. It is not their legal obligation to ensure you receive the returns on your investments that you need to fund your future dreams and goals. Further, assuming that a 401(k) portfolio will go up eventually (in the "long-run") is not good enough. You can do better.

3. Past Returns Don't Always Indicate Future Performance

The view that past returns support future performance is not rooted in statistical theory. The market does not have a "memory." In fact, it arguably could be described as following a random walk pattern. In other words, you are not guaranteed certain returns just because markets have returned a certain percentage over a specified period of time. Too often in conversations with common investors I hear, "In the long-run, the market will be up 8%," or "In the long-run, I will make money given historical performance." The market can appear to repeat itself over time; there are cyclical aspects to it that appear to be consistent over time. However, from a pure statistical standpoint, it is incorrect for us to say that the past is indicative of what will happen in the future.

Companies go through life stages as do countries. Using GDP price index data from The Bureau of Economic Analysis (www.bea.gov) indicates that over the period 2010 – the third quarter of 2012, U.S. GDP grew at a compound average of 1.83%. This type of growth would suggest that the US economy is in a mature growth stage. This mature growth is in sharp contrast to Brazil, Russia, India and China ("BRICs") that could see much larger growth in the next 40 years than the United States, thus making these geographies potentially more desirable from a pure appreciation potential perspective. If you invest in pure US companies over the next 20 years, two things can happen. First, you are not likely to see the same growth in your portfolio as other portfolios did 50 years ago when these companies or the US economy in general was in a different growth phase. Secondly, you could miss out on growth in the BRICs or any other country that is in a more rapid growth stage than the US by ignoring these as palpable investments. Please be careful not to fall into the trap of assuming that a good investment for you in the past will continue to be a good investment in the future. Investment prices are based on expected growth in the future, not the growth seen in years past. It is commonly said that past returns are not a guarantee of future returns. You should keep this at the forefront of your mind when you are building your investment portfolios and making related buy, sell and hold decisions. I caveat that with making sure you are comfortable with the risk of investing in foreign countries. No investment decision should be made by focusing purely on the potential return.

4. 401(k) Plan Investment Options Are Often Limited

Your company's 401(k) sponsor is not required to provide you with a complete universe of investment options — only enough to allow you to construct a diversified portfolio. There are so many available investment options beyond the 401(k) menu. Placing your retirement fate in a few mutual funds seems to be a risky choice. To be adequately prepared for the various financial scenarios that can affect you, consider a 401(k) plan as one investment option, not the only investment option. I hear of many people that are set on putting all their savings in their 401(k) plan. This scares me a bit. With this approach you are likely only going to meet your investment goals if markets increase by a required amount. Even a pure fixed income approach is not guaranteed to protect you in times of market turmoil. It is possible that if economic times are bad enough, fixed income investments could be linked to certain municipalities or companies that are not able to meet their interest obligations, thus defaulting, which negatively impacts the value of your fixed income investment. By having other investment vehicles available, one is able to better lock in value, no matter what direction the market moves. For example, you could consider using options to augment your investment performance. A financial option gives you the right (but not the obligation) to buy or sell a stock at a certain price, within a certain period of time. Using an option strategy can help you lock in a minimum return on a stock investment. Consider the following example:

Investor A buys a stock for $100. The stock rises in price to $110. If this investor wants to lock in their $10 gain, they can buy a put option on the stock at a strike price of $110. A put gives Investor A the right (but not the obligation) to sell the stock at $110. This can be thought of as establishing a floor gain of $10. If the stock goes up to $150, the investor can ignore the option and sell for $150. However if the price goes below $110, the put option can be exercised. By establishing a floor (or worst case scenario) for the return you want, you can save yourself from the situation where you hold a stock too long and lose all of your previous gains. Investor A in this case could maintain their $10 gain on the stock, even if the price goes down to $104, because this particular investor has the option to sell at $110, instead of the current market price of $104. It is the best of both worlds, because Investor A can still benefit from stock price increases, but is insured against stock price decreases. Keep in mind that there is a premium due on every option you buy; the premium on an option will depend on various factors such as the current stock price and volatility of the stock. Option trading can be expensive and there is risk that the other side to the transaction will not perform, so do not think that option trading isn't without its own perils. I merely want you to become educated on what other investment strategies are available. With your 401(k) plan, you do not have this same ability to lock in gains through a financial options strategy. Investing through a 401(k) plan is very much a long-only strategy, meaning that you are only going to benefit if prices go up. There is no recourse if prices start to go down.

5. 401(k) Plans Can't Be Your Only Savings Vehicle

Another concern I have with some people's 401(k) strategy is how it can be viewed as the only savings vehicle needed. In other words, the view of, "I have my checking account over here and my 401(k) over there, so I am good." What about an emergency fund for a rainy day? Having cash on hand can take away a lot of the financial stress that can occur if one unexpectedly loses their job, has a major medical expense, etc. It can be risky for people to put all their excess cash in a 401(k) plan and then cross their fingers hoping they don't get a flat tire or are not forced to decide on whether or not they can afford to replace the broken washing machine. If you live in Atlanta like I do, it is not a matter of if but when you will hit a pot hole and need to replace a tire. We also have those big boards on the roads that get put over pot holes before they get fixed. I have crushed a few of those in the past few years; I had the pleasure of getting two brand new tires as a result. Holding cash will earn minimal interest and a pure cash approach will not help you reach your retirement goals on their own, but allocating a small percentage of your portfolio to cash (e.g., 5% of your total investment portfolio) gives you added financial flexibility.

Holding cash helps you avoid losses during times when the market is uncertain and your 401(k) plan is losing money during economic downturns or recessions. This is called avoiding market exposure. Having a portion of your retirement in cash (or in other liquid investment holdings) gives you flexibility, something that you don't get from a 401(k) plan. It also allows you to avoid having all of your retirement savings exposed to market risk. "Liquid" is just another way of saying how quickly you can convert something into cash. Obviously, cash is the most liquid asset because it is already cash. An investment in a stock via an online trading account would be more liquid than a 401(k) plan; the cost of redeeming a 401(k) account is higher than a stock in an online trading account. This is because there are penalties associated with early redemption of your 401(k) investments.

This lack of flexibility of a 401(k) plan can be pretty crippling when life hits us with an unexpected emergency event. There is a nice tax benefit for investing in a 401(k) plan in the form of pre-tax contributions. However, to maintain that benefit, one has to generally hold their investment until they are 59 ½. If you start investing in your 401(k) plan after college, it could be over 30 years of waiting before you can redeem your investment. In a sense, it is setup to be a true long-term focused savings vehicle. I actually like that aspect of things, as I believe a patient investing approach wins out over time versus the active "day trading" strategy that racks up trading fees, eliminates the power of compounding, and ultimately leads to more taxes (401(k) plans are tax advantaged). However, the tradeoff is that the money invested in your 401(k) account is almost untouchable in the chance that you have a dire liquidity event (an event that requires cash immediately). I call it almost untouchable because you can get an early distribution from your 401(k) plan, but there are tax and penalty consequences. For example, if you get an early distribution from your 401(k), you get taxed on that amount on your current year tax return (because it was never taxed when you put it in your 401(k) in the first place), and you also will likely pay a penalty for redeeming early (10% penalty), unless you meet one of the IRC stated exceptions.

The penalty tax is pretty crippling because at 10%, it could end up wiping out all the gains you had on that portion of your 401(k) portfolio. Additionally, having to recognize the tax earlier than when you would in retirement, means you lose the economic advantage of the tax deferral. The longer you can defer taxes recognized on a portfolio, the greater the value of the portfolio in the future; I encourage investment in a 401(k) plan because of these stated advantages. However, it is wise to not invest so much in a 401(k) plan that it causes you to have so little cash available to meet daily needs or that any unexpected event will cause you to borrow or redeem your 401(k) investment early and thus negate many of the benefits of investing in a 401(k) plan.

401(k) Advantages

1. Pretax Contribution and Tax Deferral Benefits

Pretax contributions are one of the major benefits of a 401(k) plan. Essentially, what this means is that your contributions are not part of your "taxable income" when you prepare your tax return for the year. Consider the following example:

You decide you want to withhold $1,000 from your paycheck this year to deposit into your 401(k) plan. In this instance, $1,000 of your paycheck avoids federal income tax and goes directly into your 401(k) account. It is worth mentioning that this is a tax deferral, not tax avoidance. Eventually you will pay the tax when you start to make withdrawals from your 401(k) account (commonly during your retirement). As I mentioned earlier, withdrawing too early (prior to age 59 ½ in most cases) results in a penalty tax, but assuming you withdraw on time, you will have effectively delayed the tax on this $1,000 over a long period. If you were to not put $1,000 in a 401(k) account, but rather in a savings account, you would have taxable income for purposes of calculating your income taxes. For simplicity purposes you can assume that the total tax would be 35%. You would then have $650 to invest today vs. the $1,000 if you deposited money pre-tax in a 401(k) account. This is a pretty powerful benefit and a good reason to make 401(k) contributions.

As I stated earlier though, you don't want to do something just because there is a tax benefit. This tax benefit is great; if there is something that you need to purchase or another investment vehicle you want to pursue, you will need to weigh the benefits of having that $1,000 in a 401(k) account or the $650 to invest or spend freely. Your tax rate in retirement will determine the monetary impact of the tax deferral. If you get taxed at 30% right now, but will have a tax rate of 20% in retirement, putting money in your 401(k) account allows you to avoid a 30% tax today and pay a 20% tax when you redeem your 401(k) investment. This can be a significant tax savings. If your tax rate is the same today as it will be in retirement, taxes owed will be the same and thus the tax deferral will not have saved taxes, but it still will have delayed the payment of taxes, allowing your investments to grow without a tax drag. When considering the time value of money (a dollar today is worth more than a dollar tomorrow), it is still beneficial to use your 401(k) plan as a tax deferral vehicle.

Once you exhaust your full 2013 401(k) pre-tax contribution benefit of $17,500, you can still contribute to your 401(k) plan. Total contributions from all sources (including the $17,500 pre-tax contribution) are limited to the lesser of 100% of your compensation, or $51,000, in 2013. However, additional contributions over the $17,500 pre-tax cap will not have the same pre-tax benefit. If you decide to contribute $1,000, after you reach the $17,500 contribution limit, it would be like putting $650 in the 401(k) plan instead of the full $1,000 when contributing pre-tax. This is because any contribution after the pre-tax contribution limit of $17,500 must first be taxed before it can be invested. It is because of this that it is advisable to pursue other tax efficient vehicles once you reach your 401(k) contribution limit. There are other investment vehicles that will give you tax benefits, such as a Roth IRA, that you can take advantage of after you reach your 401(k) pre-tax contribution limit. You could also pursue investment opportunities that have a higher expected return or lower risk than the investment options in your 401(k) plan.

2. Matching Contributions

The majority of companies will match your 401(k) contributions up to a certain limit. For example, your company may explain that they will match every dollar you contribute up to 6% of your 401(k) contributions. This would mean that your company would put $60 of money into your 401(k) account if you put in $1,000; this is commonly referred to as the "free money" benefit of a 401(k) plan. This free money is only received if an employee contributes to a 401(k) plan. Over time your 401(k) returns will be greatly enhanced by these annual contributions from your employer. It almost acts like a dividend that can be reinvested. For example, assume that you contributed only one time to a 401(k) plan in an amount of $1,000. If you received $60 of free money from a matching contribution, and you got an average return of 5% over 30 years, here is the value of your 401(k) account compared to what you would have if you invested $800 after it was reduced by 20% in taxes:

	401(k)	Non 401(k) Investment Account
Balance after 30 years	$4,581	$3,458

The above table demonstrates two important points. First, the pre-tax benefit of investing $1,000 without being taxed on it first gives the 401(k) a strong advantage over investing using after-tax dollars in a vehicle other than a 401(k). This is primarily because in the no 401(k) scenario, you do not get $1,000 to invest; you get $1,000 less taxes. You can also see that there is a definite benefit from getting this extra money from your employer. Of the $1,123 difference between 401(k) and no 401(k), $259 of it is due to having the one-time $60 match invested over a 30 year period of time. The match is in place to give an extra incentive for employees to save earlier for their retirement by participating in the 401(k) plan.

I am seeing more companies place the responsibility on their employees to save for and fund their own retirement. This is a systemic shift from years ago when one could work for a company for 30 years, retire, and then have the company meet their needs in retirement through a rich pension plan. More and more companies are now going away from a pension plan. In a pension plan arrangement, the company essentially funds your retirement by investing their own money to generate the required return to meet your needs in retirement. It is now much more common for companies to favor 401(k) plans, which effectively places investment decisions in the hands of employees and thus takes away the burden from the companies to ensure there is enough money for their retired employees and having to manage a pension asset portfolio. This is a major change and requires us to have a better understanding of investments than ever before. As stated previously, rather than being responsible for funding their employee's retirement, a company's obligation is to now provide a retirement plan that offers adequate choices for an individual to build a diversified portfolio.

3. Reduced Administrative Burden

A third benefit of the 401(k) plan arrangement is that it alleviates some of the administrative burden that can go into investing. Your company is generally the sponsor of the plan and can also be the administrator of the plan or hire that out to a third party. You can have the peace of mind that the 401(k) plan is being updated, maintained, and scrutinized. Larger companies generally have a Plan Administration Committee that will review the performance of the 401(k) investment options to ensure that employees are getting the benefit of good fund performance. These committee members have experience with investing and are sometimes better able to hold funds accountable to performance than an individual with limited resources and influence. Generally, the investment vendor the company uses will have a nice way for you to track performance through an online account; it is typically set up in a way that makes the individual more aware of their options. Keep in mind, though, that it is not the Committee's responsibility to guarantee certain returns or fire fund managers if they have a bad year. Ultimately, if you have an immediate desire to re-allocate your money elsewhere, that is your responsibility. A Plan Administration Committee will not try to manage your portfolio for you, as that is not their obligation.

I would encourage anyone investing in a 401(k) plan to read the various fund prospectuses before investing in a particular fund. The fund prospectus is a legal document that will essentially tell you the characteristics of the fund and can give insight into the strategy of the fund, the fees the fund charges (this is huge because many people overlook the amount of fees and their impact on long-term returns), and the limitations placed on that fund. For example, if you are a very conservative investor and want to invest in a large company bond fund, you would like to know that the fund is not allowed to divert from this focus and in turn go invest in oil wells in an oil rich nation.

Investment Fundamentals

So now that you have a better understanding of 401(k) plans, it is time to discuss some investment fundamentals. For some of us, our knowledge of investments is similar to the following: There is the 'cash like one' (money market), the one that is not supposed to lose value but still did at times in the last few years (fixed income), stocks (equity), and foreign investments. To effectively construct an investment portfolio, it's important to know more about the types of available investments, how they work, and when they may be best for you.

The most conservative investment offering (after cash of course), would most likely be the money market mutual fund investment. The appeal of this type of investment is its safety and slightly higher return than putting money in a savings account at a bank. Though these investments are not legally guaranteed to maintain their value, money market mutual fund managers in practice will typically prevent investors from losing their principal. Disadvantages of money market mutual fund investments include extra fees, low returns and the inability to transact as quickly as you would if you had the cash in a savings account. There are savings accounts that pay out interest and do not have the fees that you would have with a money market account. Thus you will want to determine whether the added return of a money market mutual fund investment is worth the fees and reduced liquidity.

Fixed income is a broad universe of products with many variations. The most important thing to remember is that the fixed income investment is set up so that the investor has a predictable series of cash flows in the form of interest (assuming it is not a zero interest product) and an expectation of receiving a stated value at maturity. The principal is a common term associated with fixed income products; it is simply the initial amount of money invested. You can invest in a fixed income investment:

- At par, which means that the value at maturity is equal to your

initial invested principal;
- At a discount, which means your principal invested today is less than the value you will receive at maturity or
- At a premium, which means you pay more in principal today than what you will receive at maturity.

The following is a listing of the more common fixed income products:

- **US Treasury bonds and bills** are an example of fixed income, and they are considered much safer than corporate or local government investments. This is mainly because the US Treasury is unlikely to default on its interest and principal payment obligations; they can print money to meet their obligations, if needed. A US Treasury investment should be considered when one is looking for the lowest risk possible; the sacrifice made for taking on little risk is receiving lower returns.

- **Corporate Bonds** are one way a corporation raises money for new projects or to support its operations; they borrow from individuals or institutions. A corporation does this through what is called a bond offering. When a corporation offers bonds, it is asking for an investor's money now (the principal) and in return the corporation promises to pay interest at a stated rate, as well as return the initial principal. This is the most vanilla description of a corporate bond, as there are ways to add or subtract rights to/from the corporation or investor which will impact the performance of the bond. Potential investors should be primarily concerned with the financial stability of the corporation offering the bonds as this will impact the corporation's ability to make interest payments and return the initial principal. When a very strong corporation offers a bond it is generally considered a conservative investment.

- **Municipal Bonds** – are bonds issued by a municipality other than the United States government. This generally includes bonds issued by city or state governments. The bonds are either backed by the good faith of the government or the revenue being produced by a particular project, such as a toll road. These types of products have appeal as the interest on the bonds are free from federal taxation and may also be free from state taxation depending on what states issues the bond and where you reside. For example, if Georgia offers an opportunity to buy Georgia bonds and you live in Georgia, you will be exempt from paying federal and state taxes on the interest you earn during the year. If you lived in Delaware, you could still be eligible to purchase Georgia bonds and would be exempt from federal tax on the interest earned, but you would need to pay applicable state taxes. Because of this tax benefit, the interest income earned on municipal bonds is generally lower than the interest an investor can earn on bonds that pay taxable interest.

Fixed income investments have some risk but are generally suited for individuals that have lower risk preferences. Generally, lower risk investments are preferred by people who are in retirement (and therefore need to protect their investment account from losses) or who are uncomfortable with the idea of an investment portfolio ever losing money. Because fixed income investments are not perfectly correlated with equity investments, including equity and fixed income, investments in a portfolio can generally make a portfolio more efficient. What does this mean? It simply means that by having these two asset classes in the same portfolio, one will generally need to take less risk to achieve the same level of return as one would if they were solely investing in either one of the asset classes. This is the reason why you may have heard about the importance of diversification. I think this should be a primary goal for us as investors, minimizing risk and maximizing return.

Equity investments can mean a lot of things. Sticking with the spirit of this book, I will focus on the more common examples. Typically, you will hear an equity fund being called a small, mid or large cap fund. "Cap" stands for capitalization and is a term that describes the amount of shares that a company has outstanding (essentially how many shares are currently in investors' hands) multiplied by the current stock price. In practice, I have generally seen "small cap" equating to a company with a market capitalization of between $300 million and $2 billion. A "mid cap" company generally has market capitalization greater than $2 billion and less than or equal to $10 billion, and a "large cap" company is one with over $10 billion in market capitalization. These values will change over time, and there is some slight diversity in defining the thresholds, but this is a decent starting point for getting some context.

Thus, if a fund calls itself small cap, it is going to focus on investing money in small cap companies that it considers worthy of investment. Small cap firms generally have little cash flow and likely will not pay dividends for a while, but they give the investor the hope of higher returns than a very mature large cap firm. In general, the inherent risk of an investment lessens as you move from a small cap to large cap classification. However, the decrease in risk comes at the sacrifice of expected returns. Assuming an investor has the risk appetite for it, allocating your equity investment money across small, mid, and large cap funds can be a good way to diversify this class of investment, as well as offering the potential for a larger return. If a portfolio focuses on investing in only the largest companies in the United States, it will be relatively safer than an equity allocation focused on fledgling companies, but it will likely not have much growth potential because a lot of the larger companies are more established, mature, and often in industries that are not in a supernormal growth mode. Striking the appropriate balance of risk and return in your investments is an essential part of meeting your investment goals.

Diversification within your equity allocation is a powerful concept and it is a reason why many invest in equity mutual funds, because the assumption is that the fund manager will have a diversified approach. Take the example of investing in Company A alone vs. investing in Companies A-Z. The investment in Company A will have performance strongly tied to what happens at Company A; it will have a lot of firm specific risk. The idea behind investing in 25 other companies (B-Z), which should also be in a variety of industries (so as to avoid industry risk—the risk that an entire industry will be negatively impacted by a specific event and underperform), is to lessen the impact on your total return if one of the companies in your portfolio experiences significant losses. If you invest in 26 bank stocks, you no longer have as much firm specific risk, but you still have industry specific risk. There could be new banking regulation that comes out that hurts the potential for future growth at these banks, and then all of sudden the expected growth of your portfolio could decline, with no other investments to counteract the decline. If you sprinkle in some retail companies, utility companies and technology companies, your portfolio will be less impacted by this banking regulation. The good news overall is that you do not need to necessarily make these types of decisions. A lot of mutual funds strive for some form of diversification. The fund should explain in their prospectus the types of investments they seek. It is worth a quick read to ensure that the fund's target mix of investments is in line with your personal and risk and return preferences.

Fixed income and equity investments can also be foreign (as opposed to domestic). With investing becoming more and more global in nature, some of the barriers to entry that existed in the past have lessened. It would be a mistake for us to not consider foreign investments just because they are foreign to us. There are some countries that are developed and have strong economies with companies that could be well worth our investment because they provide added diversification to our portfolios (e.g., some events will impact the European economies that will not impact the United States). There are also other countries that are not as developed as the United States. Investing in companies or industries in these countries is sometimes considered investing in "emerging markets." Because there is the expectation for high growth in emerging markets or even frontier markets (e.g., investments in Sub Saharan African countries), there appears to be an opportunity for you to partake in that growth via your own investment.

There still are significant information barriers present and there aren't a lot of avenues to investing in these countries, making it very important that you proceed with the utmost caution before putting your money in these types of investment vehicles. Further, these investments are not in regulatory environments that face the same kind of regulatory scrutiny as we see in the United States. It is advisable to consult an investment professional before pursuing foreign investments. The emerging and frontier markets are mainly a growth play at the moment, with an associated high amount of risk. A published expected return on these types of investments may be very tempting, but you need to ensure that you have the appetite for risk that these investments require. The big investment gains in the next ten to twenty years may not be from a bounce back in the U.S. markets, but rather from the emerging and frontier market investments.

For the high net worth individual there are even more investment opportunities, such as private equity, hedge funds, or other alternative investment vehicles (e.g. distressed debt or equity). Typically, these investments are limited to accredited investors, because that allows for the investments to side-step some of the SEC registration requirements. Per the Securities and Exchange Commission, an accredited investor is an individual or individual and spouse that have greater than $1,000,000 in net worth (excluding the value of a personal residence) and/or have earned $200,000 or $300,000 (respectively) in the past two years. When you invest, you should always think about maximizing your return given the amount of risk you are assuming. A way to accomplish this goal is through investing in enough asset classes that move in different directions or are independent of one another (uncorrelated) so that you do not have cyclical returns and ultimately have less risk overall. This investment tenet is applicable to all investors and can be implemented by all to some degree. However, high capital requirements are necessary to fully embrace this strategy. Private equity and hedge fund investments generally require a minimum investment, and it is usually very large. Thus these investments are mostly designed for institutional investors. Institutional investors can be pension funds, endowments, or companies. Furthermore, these types of investments are best kept as 5-10% of one's total portfolio. Thus, if the requirement for investment is $10 million, you would need at least $100 million in investable assets to even consider this type of asset class. Again an investment advisor or CFA charterholder would be a good place to start if you have the ability to pursue these type of investments. Given that these investments are usually unregulated or subject to minimal regulation, it is easier for fraud to occur with these types of investments as opposed to a regulated mutual fund (as seen in a 401(k) plan). Beware of this type of risk, as a fund may not start out with the intent to be fraudulent, but the pressure to give the appearance of growth after a bad quarter could give the fund manager the incentive to misrepresent the performance of the fund.

Once you understand the universe of investments, it is important to understand how to determine the right mix of assets. Unfortunately, a lot of people go through this exercise without any idea of what dollar objective they are trying to meet. Either on your own, or with the help of a financial professional, it is very important to go through an analysis to determine the amount of money you will need during retirement to fund yourself throughout the rest of your life. Some could also have the goal of meeting their needs and then leaving the rest to loved ones or some type of charitable purpose.

One of the best ways to start figuring out a retirement target is to make an assumption about how many years you intend to live in retirement and the amount of money you will require each year.

This analysis should be exhaustive, because it is not meant to be a blind guess. Think about things like: property taxes, housing payments, car payments, basic living expenses, and anything special you want to do, such as traveling. Later in the book, I provide an example of how to do this calculation.

Your Overall Portfolio Construction

Allocating money to various investment options can be more like dart-throwing than a cautiously contemplated strategy. Hopefully the above investment definitions for the typical investor have proven helpful. Learning the investing language can help you feel a lot less intimidated when talking investments. The following tips will help you avoid a few common pitfalls:

- **Avoid picking a group of investments and not revisiting the allocation for a long period of time**. Under this mentality, the investor is not periodically assessing his or her portfolio to determine whether the current mix of investments continues to be in line with his or her risk, time horizon, and return preferences. In 2005, you may have decided you wanted 50% equities and 50% bonds. But today, maybe those equities have lost so much value that you now have an asset allocation of 30% equities and 70% bonds. This is referred to as asset mix drift, and it will happen naturally over time. If you have not been continually reviewing your mix, you may not notice natural drift of your portfolio and put yourself further away from reaching your financial goals.

- **Avoid limiting your investments to only companies that you recognize.** For example, you should avoid investing in Apple because you like your iPad and think it is the greatest thing ever. (I will not argue with that opinion, but it is not a reason to make an investment in a company.) Another common example is investing too much money in your employer because you know your company better than other companies, are optimistic about the company's outlook, or feel like you have the ability to influence that company's operations. When you do this, both the work of your hands and your equity investments are in that employer. So much of your financial wellbeing is tied to your company, a near perfect correlation. What happens if you work for an Enron type company, and tomorrow not only are you laid off, but all of your stock is virtually worthless? It would be devastating, and it was for many Enron folks who were in that situation. There are plenty of accounts out there from former Enron employees to serve as examples of understanding the impact of having all our potential financial wealth tied to a company's success.

- **Avoid getting too wrapped up in the day to day volatility of your investments.** Following every price change on a stock will drive you crazy, and you will never get any work done from the time the market opens to the time it closes. Generally, we rely on investments to meet some type of long-term goal, like retirement. As such, it is important to maintain a long-term perspective when it comes to the value of your investments. If you watch a financial news channel every day, the bad news would be enough to make you want to bury your money in a clay pot somewhere. Bad news sells. Unfortunately, it is better "water cooler" talk to say "Man, did you see the market today? It is getting killed — down another 300 points!" A bad day or week for the S&P 500 should not cause us to think about changing our allocation or selling off our investments. This is not to mean you should have static portfolios. Focus at the onset on developing your unique strategic asset allocation and then change that mix when circumstances related to your life change, extreme market events call for a change, or a market change has been so drastic that your initial strategic allocation is no longer relevant to you.

The market goes up and it goes down — it is inherently volatile. In practice, I rarely hear people complain about the market going up, but usually I hear a lot of negative comments when the market goes down. In the long-run, equity markets have shown an ability to increase, and that should be the mentality that helps us keep our sanity when a bad month or two happens. I would advise against looking at your investment values daily. Reviewing your portfolio quarterly is good enough. This time frame is long enough to prevent us from making a hasty decision based on temporary volatility, but short enough to allow us to detect significant shifts in our portfolio away from our strategic asset allocation intentions. Day trading, in my opinion, will more times than not, just lead to a lot of trading costs and non-beneficial tax treatment should the day trader be fortunate enough to gain on their investments.

After a healthy discussion of 401(k) plans and investments fundamentals, it is helpful to bring this together by talking about your overall portfolio construction, of which your 401(k) plan can be an integral part. Regarding portfolio construction, how many people actually look at all their cash and investments as one portfolio? More likely, you will look at your bank account and say I have X for my bills, I have Y for my general expenses during the month, and Z is what is left over (you hope!). You then move to our savings account and might say that a portion of that is for a rainy day, or it could be for your children's education or a charitable purpose. Next we move to your investment account. But this may all be done in complete isolation.

This is the perfect point to pause and think about how you have divided up your resources. Take the following scenario. If you have $10 in your checking account, $10 in your savings account and $80 in your investment account ($40 in equities and $40 in bonds), what is your allocation to equities? If you said 40%, you are correct. Some people may have answered 50%, arguing that equities are 50% of their investment account. If you wanted a 50% allocation to equities, you should have had $50 in equities and $30 in bonds, because you have $100 in total assets. I fear that too many of us are looking at our investment account in isolation from the rest of our available assets. You should start to think about all of your investable assets in unison and then put that in the context of your risk, time horizon, and return needs. If the above example were for a 25 year old with a propensity for higher risk, a 40% equity allocation would probably be too low, given this individual has potentially 40 more working years to build his or her retirement portfolio. Even more interesting, this 25 year old may incorrectly think they have a 50% allocation to equities.

Determining Your Risk Tolerance and Required Return

Once you have decided on what you need to save for retirement, your reliable spreadsheet, calculator or CFP® professional will then provide you with the return you are required to generate on your current investment account to reach that investment objective. I also provide a sample calculation later in the book for your reference. I implore you to be realistic when determining the desired size of your investment portfolio. If you need a 15% return to meet your retirement needs, but have no desire to take any risk, one of two things need to change: you either need to change your spending requirement during retirement (as it's likely too high,) or you need to be willing to accept more risk. Think of it this way — the passage to higher return usually is on the road of risk. It is important to honestly assess your risk tolerance. Some financial planners will give you a questionnaire of non-financial scenarios aimed at determining your overall tolerance for risk. You can also find these types of questionnaires on the internet. Typically, non-financial questions are asked in these questionnaires because through use of these types of questions it is easier to see how you view risky situations. For example, there could be a question like, "How likely would you be to sky dive on a scale of 1-10, 10 being the highest?" A well-built questionnaire should reveal your propensity for risk taking, which will be a starting point for determining how much risk you are comfortable accepting when investing. If you typically accept a high level of risk, have a long time horizon, and have a high return requirement, then you probably have a high level of risk tolerance, and thus could potentially invest in choices such as foreign equities. Conversely, if you describe yourself as having a low willingness to accept risk, a short time horizon, and low return requirement, then it would signal a conservative investment approach.

If you determine that you have average risk tolerance, a medium time horizon (15-20 years), and a return objective of 8%, it could support a portfolio that has a nice mix of equities and fixed income, with the equity investments being mostly mature (large cap investments), with a small focus on foreign investments. Something like 60% equities (40% U.S. Domestic large cap, 10% mid cap, 5% small cap, 5% Foreign) and 40% fixed income (100% U.S. Domestic fixed income) could be a reasonable allocation. As we slide that scale toward higher risk tolerance, there could be a shift into equities of as high as 80%, with more focus on foreign and small cap investments, less emphasis on fixed income, and possibly a small investment in an alternative strategy. Of course you can also decrease your risk tolerance by sliding your equity exposure to 30-40%, loading up on fixed income products at 50-60%, and perhaps having a small portion in cash (5%-10%). There are no bright lines or right numbers to use when allocating, so don't spend a ton of time debating whether your equity exposure should be 35% or 36%. Below is an illustration of the various potential portfolio allocation possibilities. It is not meant to be authoritative, but rather merely for visual purposes. Your own personal allocation should be based on your risk and return preferences.

High Risk/Return Example

Portfolio Allocation

- Alternatives 11%
- Fixed Income 5%
- Small Cap Equities 17%
- Large Cap Equities 67%

The above allocation could be desirable for the individual that is:
- Young and thus has a long investment horizon;
- Would be labeled as a risk taker on a risk questionnaire;
- Has a lot of money to invest and therefore has a need to diversify across many asset classes; and/or
- Has an aggressive retirement or other investment goal, thus requiring high investment returns.

Normal Risk/Return Example

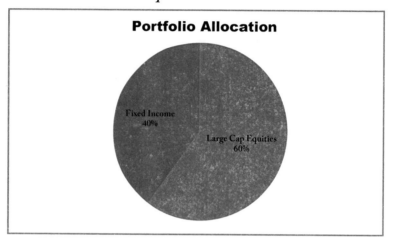

The above allocation could be desirable for the individual that is:
- Approaching their 40's and thus has a medium term investment horizon;
- Would be labeled as an average to slightly above average risk taker on a risk questionnaire; and/or
- Has a retirement or other investment objective that requires a stronger tilt towards the higher returns that equity investments offer.

Low Risk/Return Example

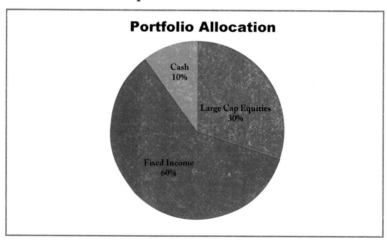

The above allocation could be desirable for the individual that is:

- Approaching retirement and thus has a need for more liquid investments or investments that will preserve their value in the immediate term;
- Would be labeled as a below average risk taker on a risk questionnaire; and/or
- Has a retirement or other investment objective that is close to being funded through their investment portfolio and therefore is not motivated by chasing the higher returns offered by equity investments.

Whatever you decide, you need to ensure that you are realistic and understand that there is a relationship between risk and return. If risk makes you nervous, and you can't stand the thought of losing money, it is perfectly fine, but you need to understand that you may not have a bountiful retirement funded by gigantic investment returns. There is no canned answer for everyone. Do not read this section, think you are average risk and set up an allocation of 60% equity and 40% fixed income without further analysis.

Each person needs to know the range of what his or her required dollar amount is to have in retirement or to achieve some other investment objective, the required return to get there, and the risk accepted to get to that destination.

These factors should reconcile appropriately, meaning that if you think you need millions of dollars in retirement but are running with a fixed income portfolio, something does not make sense or reconcile, and revisiting your approach is advisable. Once you get these answers, your strategic asset allocation will become clearer. Obviously, someone who has no ability to take risks (e.g., they have a lot of debt or other expenses and can't afford serious investment losses), may not be able to accept a lot of risk. With a person who has a high expectation for their portfolio's dollar value but is unwilling to ever invest in equity investments, it follows that this person may not see the returns needed to meet their investment objectives.

Putting It All Together

After learning about all the types of investments, risk and return concepts, and asset mix methodology, you may be wondering, how do I use this new found knowledge? Employer sponsored defined contribution plans are required to give investors some basic knowledge so that they can make informed decisions on which investments to select. However, your employer is not responsible for giving you investment advice, and in fact, is not supposed to do so. Many of the large 401(k) vendors have the expertise and software to guide you through how to select a reasonable asset mix based on your risk and return preferences. Keep in mind, though, that those vendors will want you to invest in their products, so you may not get the most unbiased guidance.

A professional money manager (I'd look for a CFA charterholder or CFP® professional if possible) is also an option for those who have more investable assets than the 401(k) contribution limit or do not participate in a 401(k) or other defined contribution plan. These individuals will be able to give you a more personalized plan than would be available through a 401(k) plan as these professional money managers should be looking to get you the best execution of any investment that fits within your risk and return profile. You will usually pay a management fee for these services. If you select this route, make sure you are meeting with your money manager on a quarterly basis so that you can evaluate their performance after accounting for the fees you are paying the manager for their services. Both you and the money manager should probably agree on a benchmark ahead of time so that you have a meaningful way to measure the money manager's performance. A common benchmark for an investment portfolio that is invested in the largest companies in the US would be the S&P 500. If the S&P 500 was up 7% for the quarter but your money manager only made you 1% for the quarter after deducting his or her fees, an explanation for the shortfall would be warranted.

You could also do all this yourself, using an online trading platform. There are no doubt people that make money "day trading." You can take all your money, do your own research and build your own portfolio using the principles in this book. However, in the long run, even the best financial professionals in the world don't consistently beat the market after expenses. If you are going to invest on your own, and it is consistent with your return and risk preferences, I would consider using index funds or exchange traded funds ("ETFs"). Many ETFs attempt to mimic a certain index, such as an S&P 500 ETF. By investing in an S&P 500 ETF, you are investing in a product that is attempting to copy the performance of the S&P 500. The ETF product universe is so expansive now that you can find an ETF for pretty much anything, whether it be fixed income, equities, real estate, or even commodities (such as gold). Investing in an ETF keeps your investment expenses down because ETFs have a more efficient expense structure than traditional mutual funds. Investing in an ETF also allows you to invest in a diversified product, rather than having to worry about buying a lot of different stocks and trying to achieve diversification on your own. I also favor ETFs because they can be used to easily get exposure to various types of asset classes, some of which have barriers to entry.

Concluding Remarks

There are undoubtedly many other investment questions to answer. If I could, I would meet personally with everyone who reads this book to discuss these topics so I could provide more detail on what investment strategy works for you. I could talk about options, shorting stocks, or anything else that you would find interesting. The purpose of this section is to avoid being too detailed or technical in order to stick with the book's express purpose, which is to take financial concepts that we all face and put them in non-business school terms. I did not want this section to turn into a textbook on investing, and if it has, there is no doubt some drool on these pages right now. Most of all, I wanted this section to not be intimidating. It is my hope that everyone who reads this book will become capable enough to get a handle on this area of their life; at a minimum I want the readers of this book to participate in an intelligent conversation with someone that they hired to handle the investing aspect of their lives. Sometimes we just need to have things explained a certain way, then it clicks, we feel equipped, and can move onward and upward!

Retirement Planning Principles

How will I know when I am safe to retire? I think it is safe to assume that this is a question many people ask themselves. It has even prompted recent commercials wherein two people text back and forth regarding their retirement, with the conclusion always being an open ended question that seems to go unanswered. Retirement can mean different things for different people. For one person it could just mean quitting his or her current profession and working on a more part-time or flexible basis. Others may want to pursue some type of community service initiative. The possibilities are truly endless, but at some point the majority of you will want to have enough money to have the flexibility to set your own schedule and perhaps pursue something you have always wanted to do, but never felt like you had the time or ability to do. It is this very thing that causes thousands every year to seek out financial advice.

To help you plan for retirement, a financial professional will typically go through a planning process that involves the following key steps:

- Determine how much you expect to spend during retirement;
- Understand your current and future sources of retirement income; and
- Identify the financial decisions you should consider to help you reach your goals.

In the previous chapter, you learned about investment strategies. Investments usually play an important role in a sound retirement plan, so it will be important to remember the investment principles presented earlier so that you can determine whether your investments will cover your expected spending during retirement. You may be wondering why we would focus on trying to project your retirement expenses first. Retirement is not like your working years where you get a paycheck and just spend it until the next paycheck. It is a much more deliberate process that requires meticulous planning. If you don't have a clue how much you will project to spend during your retirement, it will be very hard to know much money you need to save and invest today.

How Much Do You Expect to Spend During Retirement?

Before you can contemplate the dollar range of what you will need in retirement, (and let me stress, it should be a range, not a "number"), it is important to come up with a detailed plan of what you expect to spend in retirement. I like to call this our "goal range." This is called funding your retirement. There is no way for you to get an accurate read of what you will need to save for retirement unless you try to forecast your expenditures in retirement. Thus, you should have a goal for what you want in retirement, and the best way to plan is to have a well thought out goal range. The more seriously you take this exercise, the narrower and more predictable your range of expected expenses in retirement becomes. A good model for performing this exercise is to list expected expenses and break them down between necessary and goal expenses. Necessary expenses are basic needs items such as food, health care, and housing; goal expenses are items such as buying a second house, making a large charitable contribution, or trying to leave a target inheritance for future generations. This exercise requires an honest assessment because it will be the driver for the amount of money you will need to have in your retirement portfolio when you stop generating your former income from your occupation. Once you determine the total necessary expenses you will have each year of your retirement, you can table your expected annual expenses (adjusted for inflation) in the following accepted manner:

Age	Expenses Before Adjustment (A)	Probability Of Reaching Age (B)	Expenses Per Year (A*B)
65	$60,000	99%	$59,400
66	$63,000	98%	$61,740
67	$66,150	97%	$64,166
68	$69,458	96%	$66,680
69	$72,930	95%	$69,284
70	$76,577	94%	$71,982

The above table assumes a single individual retiring at age 65. Further, it assumes that expenses will grow at a rate of 5% each year due to an estimated increase in the cost of living. Lastly, a probability of reaching each age is applied to the expenses before adjustment column to get a required expense amount for each age in retirement. This is typically called a mortality assumption. You can build this calculation out through any age you desire. You can also run this calculation by including your goal expenses. These two numbers will represent the dollar range of expected expenditures in retirement in future value dollar terms.

The expenses before adjustment column increases each year by an assumed rate of inflation (this calculation assumes 5%). The total future value of the above calculation is $393,252 (merely a sum of the amounts in the expenses per year column). If I convert this amount to a present value on the date of your retirement using a 5% discount factor, it converts to a need of $347,401 (using the NPV function on a financial calculator) on the day you reach 65. Assume you turn 40 today and want to make your first retirement savings deposit today. You will need to make 25 annual payments of approximately $5,133 (assuming a 7% growth rate on your account balance) to reach your retirement goal on the day you reach age 65. This is a bit simplified, as the goal is to have a longer retirement than the six years in this example, but it illustrates the mechanics of the retirement needs calculation and also demonstrates how important it is to start early when saving for retirement. If you are receiving Social Security or pension benefits, you will want to approximate the present value of those benefits as it reduces the amount of money you will need each year in retirement from your investment portfolio. This calculation can get complex and subjective, and thus it is probably best to discuss your particular situation with a financial professional. At the very least, you now have a basic idea of how to calculate the amount you will need in retirement. For now just understand how important it is to project the expenses you expect to have in retirement and then find a means to reach those goals based on your required return and risk preferences.

Things To Remember When Calculating Your Retirement Expenses

Now that you've learned the general process for determining your expected retirement expenditures, there are some other considerations you should keep in mind to further develop this calculation.

Most individuals look to investments to meet their retirement needs. According to data compiled by a professor at NYU named Aswath Damodaran, US stocks had a geometric average return of 9.23% over the period 1928 – 2011. Because your retirement portfolio will not always be 100% weighted to equities, you could use 7% as a reasonable starting point for a rate of return to expect on your retirement savings from the date you start saving until your retirement. However, please understand that just because the return on US stocks over the last 84 year period of time was 9.23% does not mean that there will be another 9.23% return in the next 84 year period. The return assumption of 7% should be further adjusted downward if you are a much more conservative investor and rely heavily on fixed income. In that case, you could consider using 4% as the rate of return on your retirement savings up until retirement. It probably would be advisable to get a financial professional involved with this calculation as it could give you the peace of mind that you have calculated a reasonable retirement goal range. If you want to try it yourself, I recommend purchasing a financial calculator and doing an internet search on how to perform time value of money calculations.

Calculating a reasonable retirement goal range requires a thoughtful process. The point of this chapter is to bring awareness to how you should think about calculating the amount of money you will need in retirement. There is a degree of subjectivity in this calculation, but there is a method that can be used to make you feel more comfortable with seeing how close you are to meeting your retirement goals. Even if you are not doing the calculation, challenge your financial advisor to explain how they developed their retirement target range so that you can feel more a part of the process.

The key components of this process are:

- Come up with a reasonable expenditure assumption during your retirement;
- Establish the amount of money you can afford to put in savings each year toward your retirement goal; and
- Determine what type of risk you are willing to take with that savings to meet your retirement goal.

This is not a static practice. Life happens, which is another way of saying, sometimes things happen in life that are unexpected, and cause us to pause and adjust our plan. I would recommend having a meeting with a financial professional at least annually to review the retirement goal range assumptions that were developed during your initial retirement savings discussion. If you are performing this calculation yourself, I would recommend that you review your assumptions quarterly. It is so easy to communicate these days. Do not wait until your quarterly or annual meeting with your financial advisor if you face a significant decision or have had a major life change; email or pick up the phone immediately. Sometimes a proactive discussion with a financial advisor can save you the pain of finding out later that you could have done "X" instead of "Y" and now you adversely impacted your retirement nest egg as a result.

It is preferred practice to establish a goal range, with there being a floor amount (the amount you absolutely need to have to eat and have shelter) and a ceiling amount that would be achieved if you were able to save more per year than expected and/or of your investment portfolio performed a lot better than expected. The high end of the goal range would include the amount that you need to get your dream house, start your dream business, or whatever endeavor you have in your heart to pursue that will require above a comfortable state of living. At a minimum, you will want to get into retirement with enough money so that you do not need to go back to working a job to meet basic living needs. The low end of your retirement range needs to be well thought out to the point where there is a very slim likelihood that basic needs will not be met for the duration of your retirement. As mentioned earlier, you need to make sure that basic needs do not include things like eating out at nice restaurants every week and buying other luxury goods. If you want those types of things, you can build them into your goal range, but allowance for these types of expenditures should be at the upper end of the range rather than at the very low end of the range.

The floor/ceiling goal range calculation and related goal range can be further enhanced if you have a desire to have a certain amount of money left over when you pass away. Up until this point, I have assumed that the objective is to calculate a goal range that will meet your needs from retirement until death. No doubt there are individuals that want their money to outlast them and then perhaps be used as an inheritance for the next generation or a charitable purpose (to name a few). The good news is that there are other mechanisms to fund the needs of the next generation if you do not want to build that into your goal range. For example, a life insurance policy should be a part of our retirement planning decision, as a life insurance policy can help you achieve the objective to leave money to your beneficiaries so that your retirement savings can focus on funding your retirement that you have worked so hard to enjoy.

To summarize the five points above:

- Carefully consider your expected retirement portfolio return;
- Be deliberate and realistic when determining your retirement goal range;
- Revisit your retirement goal range regularly;
- Establish a firm floor and ceiling amount for your retirement; and
- Adjust your retirement goal range if you intend to leave a bequest.

Are Annuities Right For You?

Maybe your concern is not leaving money for beneficiaries, but rather having a dependable stream of payments throughout the rest of your life. A retirement tool that serves that purpose is the annuity. The annuity is an exciting option because it provides a stream of payments at a certain point of time in our life (you can decide when annuity payments begin) for the remainder of our life or for a designated period of time. An annuity can be set up so that the annuity:

- Makes payments for a fixed period of time;
- Is a fixed amount until the payments run out (if someone dies with the annuity payments still due, they pass on to the stated beneficiary until the annuity balances zeroes out);
- Makes payments for the remainder of your life; or
- Makes payments for the remainder of your life and the life of a beneficiary.

This takes a lot of the guesswork out of what to expect in retirement, by providing you a stream of payments you can count on to cover your retirement needs. The amount of the payments can vary, and they are based in part on the payments you make into the annuity during the annuity funding period, as well as the performance of the investments invested in or the stated interest rate on the annuity. An annuity is pretty simple. First, you sign-up for the annuity and can either make a single payment up front or make regular payments to an annuity provider for a stated period of time. A common annuity arrangement is one whereby you make annuity payments from the day you enter into the annuity until retirement (or the end of the funding period). At this point you will stop paying the annuity; it will start paying you. The payments received are greater than the payments you made because the annuity has grown in value. While the annuity is growing, the unrealized earnings are not taxable to you either.

Types of Annuities

There are two basic types of annuities — the fixed annuity and the variable annuity. The fixed annuity has a stated rate of return on the payments you make into the annuity, so you can be fairly certain what to expect in retirement. It is similar to the fixed income investment I discussed in the investments section. The variable annuity has a rate of return that is dependent on the investments made while your payments build up into the annuity. Think of this annuity as being akin to the equity type of investment that was discussed in the investment section. The variable annuity has more risk than the fixed annuity because it does not have a guaranteed return, but it has an upside that a fixed annuity lacks. Given that in the long-term, equity markets have performed well, a variable annuity, despite its uncertain return, could be a good option for those willing to take on a little more risk for the chance at a higher annuity payout in the future. Please keep in mind that despite having annuity in its description, the variable annuity can lose money, and thus should not be used if one is risk averse.

In Summary

This chapter has some overlap with the chapter on investments in that the understanding gained in the investments section and your use of investments will have a strong influence on your retirement plan. Your retirement goal range will be strongly impacted by your or your financial advisor's understanding of investment concepts and the related investment returns.

When thinking about your retirement, it's important to remember the following key concepts:

- Honestly assess your needs in retirement, separating needs from desires.
- Learn how to calculate or have a financial planner aid you in calculating your retirement goal range.
- Know your appetite for risk and make sure it is aligned with your retirement goal range. A retirement goal range that is only possible for the biggest risk taker is likely not appropriate for someone that is very conservative.

Following these key concepts will help you set a goal, which is a very important step in retirement planning. A goal will give you direction and awareness of what you are trying to achieve, as well as a way to monitor over time whether you are on track to achieve your goal.

Debt Principles

Debt is something we are all familiar with to some extent. I have yet to talk with someone who enjoyed making debt repayments, unless of course it is the last debt repayment. There are varying views regarding debt. There are financial institutions that can make a lot of money off getting people into debt, so there is fervor in that circle toward the concept of debt. Of course, when too many people get money that they cannot pay back, bad things can occur. (Subprime loan crisis anyone?) On the other hand, there is a camp that completely swears off all debt and argues that our chief financial focus should be avoiding debt. Some investors will use short-term debt to aggressively pursue an investment opportunity they think will produce significant returns. Others use small business debt because they have an idea they believe in and need the capital to get the idea off the ground. Some would not be able to go to college if it were not for loans. Knowing all of this, where does one side on the issue of debt? Is it ever good? Is it always bad? How can I tell the difference?

Personally, I think that the answer is not so black and white. Clearly there is bad debt, mostly consumer driven, which is a result of people's inability to delay gratification. I would never approve of someone who goes into debt to "invest" in the latest fashions. On the other side, though, is it wrong for a person to chase a lifelong business dream which requires a little debt to make the initial investment? Answering that question is a lot harder. To get us thinking about debt in general, I divided this chapter into Good Debt and Bad Debt, and each sub section of this chapter discusses some examples of each. The division is not intended to make this a black and white issue, because it is not always easy to draw the line, but rather to think about the motivation and ultimate goal associated with the debt. If the motivation for the debt is wrong and the ultimate goal does not have a payoff greater than the cost to borrow, it is usually a bad idea. A quick rule of thumb for how you can categorize your debt would be the following:

If debt is for investment, it can be good. If debt is for consumption, it is likely bad.

Good Debt

The decision to apply for debt is one of the more serious financial decisions you will make. A portion of Proverbs 22:7 reads, "the borrower is slave to the lender,"(New International Version) and I could not agree more. The first thing you need to figure out is whether you think you will be better off financially after the debt is paid off than you were before you applied for the debt. This can typically be measured in two ways. If you are trying to determine whether to borrow money to build a business or buy a stock, the return on the business or stock needs to be greater than the interest rate on your loan plus any other fees (and there will be some for sure) you pay associated with that loan. Another way to look at the benefit of a loan is whether you are better off professionally or financially as a result of the loan. This can be harder to measure, but imagine the following situation:

Scenario A: Individual decides not to borrow to go to a top 10 rated university and goes to another accredited university instead, deciding to pay cash for college. This individual ends up with career earnings of $2,000,000 and college education expenses of $20,000 for a $1,800,000 net.

Scenario B: An individual of similar ability takes a loan to go to a top 10 university. This individual does well in school and has access to some of the top jobs in the country. This individual ends up with career earnings of $5,000,000 and combined interest and education expenses of $250,000 for a $4,750,000 net. As you can see, the difference is significant and of course assumes that the individual does not do anything after his/her undergraduate program to further augment his/her career potential. For some, the same analysis will likely need to be done to determine whether it makes sense to take out a loan for a graduate program. It is for this reason that I do not like to assume that student loan debt is a bad thing. Rare is the person who can bring thousands of dollars to the table to pay for an undergraduate or graduate degree. Further, student loans typically have a much lower rate of interest than other forms of debt and can be fixed at low rates. Student loans usually do not become due until a student finishes school, so it is less burdensome in that regard as well. Also, student loan interest is deductible for tax purposes at certain income levels.

The scenarios above are simplistic, but they are intended to illustrate the amount of thought that needs to go into whether to borrow money or not. Having a mindset that all debt is bad could have prevented the person in Scenario B from ever attaining a lifetime goal to go to a top 10 university and have the career earnings that they always envisioned. At the same time, borrowing a lot of money to go to a school because it has beautiful weather would not qualify as a great reason to take out a lot of debt to go to school, especially if a lower priced alternative would provide the same potential earnings potential or get that person a degree of similar or better quality.

The recent economic downturn has made it more difficult for graduates to find jobs after school. No longer can you hand an employer proof of a college diploma and expect to be hired. Borrowing for school must be strategic and students at school should have a plan from day one on how to ensure that they will be able to pay their student loans once they graduate (e.g., find a job before graduation). Student loans are not dischargeable in bankruptcy and thus do not go away if you lack money to pay them. Typically, student loans start becoming due six months after graduation (though some student loans charge deferred interest from the time the money is borrowed to the time the first payment is due, leading to an even larger debt balance). Obviously, your children are not going to have student loan payments on the top of their priority list when they attend school. However, they can contribute to managing this family loan by being proactive in school: getting good grades, internships, and finally, securing a job before graduation. This is one example that supports why whenever I am asked about the topic of debt and whether one should have debt; my standard answer is "it depends."

Another common debt scenario we face is whether to apply for a mortgage to buy a house. Buying a home and the related entrance costs makes it incredibly difficult to avoid some form of borrowing. How easy is it to go to the seller of a home and write them a check for hundreds of thousands of dollars? Rather than try to do this, it may be more beneficial for you to think about how much sense it makes to borrow when buying a home and, probably more importantly, how much you really need to spend on that home. I hope that after reading this book you will become a developed saver of money, and thus be able to lower the amount of debt required to buy a home. After reading this book, if you have learned to delay gratification and develop a mature understanding of your needs, the house you choose now may be smaller and less expensive than you would have chosen otherwise. Debt is a burden in its own right, but it's also important to avoid getting a house that is way above your needs and not only creates a burden in terms of the monthly mortgage payment, but also in terms of the upkeep of the house. As much as you want to believe it will make you happy, a house will never make you happy. It is not designed to fill your heart with joy, it is designed to serve as shelter for you and those you care about. If you go to the mortgage table with the mentality of "house as shelter," you will be much better off in the long run.

Once you make a mature decision about the house you want to buy, you need to understand the debt options at your disposal. A common option is the 30 year fixed rate mortgage.

The 30 year mortgage can be tricky, especially in times of low rates, because the length of the payment cycle can convince you that you can afford a bigger, more expensive house than is prudent.

When you go to a bank or call a bank over the phone, they can quickly calculate the monthly payments required on the 30 year loan. It is so tempting to immediately think, "Yes, I can pay that, sign me up!" A mortgage can easily slide onto the bad debt side of the ledger when you borrow to buy a house that you can technically afford, but don't really need. As I mentioned earlier, it is time to challenge whether you view a house the same way you view other types of investments. Keep in mind that a house is an investment that is illiquid, unique, and requires physical upkeep. Also, as we have seen in the past few years, house prices are not guaranteed to go up in value or even maintain value. This is troublesome as so many individuals have their personal wealth tied to a house and are suffering as a result of housing price declines. Given this, I think borrowing to buy a house should be viewed differently than borrowing to buy a stock or to invest in a well planned business venture. (This excludes pure speculation or blind investment based on a friend's "hot tip".) If you are taking a mortgage on a house because it has all the things you want (customized rooms) versus the things you need (basic housing and shelter), then a mortgage can be very similar to consumer credit card debt. If you are a family of four, I would challenge you to consider whether you need 4,000 square feet. Always consider how much cash you can put down on a house and how much of your bi-weekly take home pay will have to be used to make your monthly mortgage payments. After making these considerations it's worth asking yourself whether you can really afford the house you desire. If so, that is excellent. This section is not about telling people that have a lot of money not to buy things they can afford. Rather, it is about encouraging people not to borrow to buy something they truly cannot afford.

As a good rule of thumb, I generally do not like to see a housing payment be more than 25% of gross income.

Using this concept will force you to live within your means and also protect you from situations such as being without a job for a few months and being dependent on savings to meet mortgage payments. Please let me reiterate: I have no fundamental problem with people buying things they can afford (and this book is not about trying to make people feel guilty for buying nice stuff that they can afford). Rather, mortgages concern me when they are used for more than meeting our basic needs of shelter and protection by people that cannot comfortably afford to have extra luxuries. The primary issue, and what makes a mortgage turn from good debt to bad debt, is when people take out a mortgage on a house they can barely afford. Then when something goes wrong and they can no longer or can barely afford it, it causes so much stress that it starts to ruin their relationships with the people around them. It can also lead to short sales, foreclosures, and ruined credit.

It is to your advantage to be honest with yourself when you are deciding on buying a new house. What is your true motivation? Is it to provide a safe shelter for your family or is it to impress your friends or family? Do you really need to move houses because you need to make room for your newborn baby? If 1,000 square feet was enough for you and your wife before, does having a newborn 7 pound, 7 ounce baby who cannot move around require you to move immediately? In today's environment, a large down payment (10-20%) at the time of purchase is becoming the standard; lenders have more stringent restrictions on which applicants they will approve for a home loan and how much money they can lend out. As such, you should plan on having at least 20% in cash savings towards a down payment.

Do not redeem your 401(k) money to pay for a house unless it is an absolute emergency prior to applying for a mortgage. Perhaps you should consider holding yourself to a different standard, in the sense that your mortgage down payment should not completely wipe out your savings. If a down payment on a house leaves you with no savings, you are simply not ready to make a home purchase. Renting a house for a season of your life is okay, especially if by renting you position yourself to buy a house when you are in a more stable financial condition.

I am recommending you be disciplined enough to ensure that your down payment on a new home will not exceed 50% of your savings. I recommend this guideline because it is my aim that when you sign off on your mortgage, you still have enough money to continue building on your retirement, saving for college, or merely having an adequate cash reserve in case a once in a lifetime opportunity comes your way. I would hate for buying a house to be such a burden that it causes you to rebuild your savings from zero. Burden is a keyword in that last sentence. The mortgage in itself is not so bad, but it can be if it is a burden for you to pay monthly, or causes you to miss out on other attractive profit opportunities. Another reason I like having 50% of savings remaining after closing on a new home is that there is little certainty about whether the value of a home will go up or down. The housing market over the last four years taught us the valuable lesson that housing prices can decline at any time and stay down for extended periods of time. No doubt you or someone you know has a mortgage that is underwater. Imagine how much stress would be produced in a scenario where you put all your money down on a house, the house declines sharply in value, and then you need to sell it in three years to take a job in another location. It may be difficult or even impossible to sell that house without any additional money in savings. Faced with this unfortunate but now common situation, you will be forced to bring more cash to the closing table if you desire to sell. If you haven't been diligent in saving money, an underwater mortgage could force you to agree to a short sale or foreclosure, both of which have a disastrous impact on future credit.

Lastly, you should understand the risk of having so much of your funds available for investment tied up in a house. I am concerned that too many people view their house as their primary investment vehicle. If your entire investable assets were worth $100,000 (investments + cash in your savings and checking accounts) and you decided to make a $30,000 down payment on a house, 30% of your investment portfolio would be weighted in real estate. Do your risk and return preferences allow for a 30% allocation to real estate? You should ask yourself this question before you take all your cash savings and plow them into a down payment on a house. When real estate becomes such a large portion of your investment allocation that it exceeds your personal investment risk tolerance, the associated leverage could be viewed as bad debt.

Below is a summary of key mortgage takeaways:

- Ensure that a mortgage down payment is 50% or less of your savings.
- Ensure that your monthly mortgage payment is not greater than 25% of your gross monthly income.
- Be prepared to put 20% down towards your home purchase.
- Do not get into a loan with the expectation that you will be able to refinance. I made this mistake when I bought my first house and was unable to refinance out of a high interest loan.
- Honestly assess your motivation for buying a home. A mortgage can be akin to a large credit card balance if you get a house for the wrong reasons.
- Evaluate what percentage your down payment on a mortgage is in relation to the sum of your total cash and other investments.

You should have a complete understanding of how your debt will impact your life going forward. If possible, you never want to take out debt of any kind if a slight change in your circumstances will cause you to have trouble making repayments. If you are thinking certain debt can work for you because you have an overly optimistic projection for how your life is going to be throughout the duration of the loan, you should force yourself to think of a more balanced outcome, choosing to also consider whether the loan would make sense if one of your family members lost a job or started working part-time. Risk management is essential when you are making a borrowing decision; you should consider the potential for bad outcomes in the future and whether you can make debt repayments under the worst of circumstances. Whether debt is good or bad for you will likely depend on your own individual situation. Also, you need to look at your debt in total and not just in isolation. You could make a good business case for why each loan makes sense individually, but once you start to aggregate the debt, the repayments may prove burdensome.

If greater than 36% of your gross income is being used to pay back loans, you are likely over levered.

There is some debt, though, that you should avoid entirely, and I will discuss that next — it is called "Bad Debt" and it is the enemy of all that strive for a strong financial plan.

Bad Debt

There is clearly a dark side to debt, and the general theme that makes it so is when individuals get tempted to, and start to, borrow above their means on things they do not really need. Usually I see this happen through the three bad debt amigos:

- Credit card debt
- Car loans
- Pledging equity as collateral for a personal expense

The easiest way to borrow above your means is via the credit card. Credit cards have their fans. I could sit down with someone right now and they could tell me about all the points they have received by using credit cards and how they always pay their bill on time. I would congratulate that person and be happy for them, but it wouldn't change my view on whether using a credit card creates bad debt. For everyone that successfully plays the system and gets points and never has interest payments, there are plenty more that have gone in the negative and are now on the "pay the minimum" month to month plan. Credit cards are not in the business to issue you "free credit." Save yourself the trouble, and don't use credit cards. I have lived the credit card nightmare while I was a college student and can tell you that receiving the constant phone calls, enduring the threatening letters and ultimately settling with the credit card company (which negatively impacted my credit for years) was an experience I have no desire to repeat. Credit card companies would not stay in business if everyone made their payments on time and earned tons of points on their purchases. There are people out there that are in deep enough debt that their interest payments are funding the credit card company's points programs and contributing to the profitability of the credit card company.

Using credit cards is among the easiest ways to risk having your total expenditures exceed your income. If you imagine a world where you could only spend what you possessed, at worst, expenditures would equal your income, and at best, your income would significantly exceed your expenditures. In my past, I have certainly used credit cards to my advantage by saving the money I could use to make a purchase and instead paying with a credit card, which allowed me to invest my savings, pay off my credit card bill later and hope to get a return on the cash I invested during the interim period. In today's environment, short-term rates on fixed income investments are so low and investing in equities is so risky that at best, you earn a miniscule return by floating the payment, and at worst, you lose money on your short-term equity investment and need to pay more money than previously to settle your credit card bill.

I bring this example up not as an endorsement of this strategy, but to illustrate that even though I understand the concept of floating payments, I don't teach it as a fundamental for financial responsibility. For every person that games the credit card system by earning lots of points or successfully floating payments, there are many others that got too aggressive with their charge card, or were not disciplined enough, and ended up in a debt position they struggled or are still struggling to overcome. So much of life is about habits. Continually spending with a credit card creates the bad habit of spending more than you possess. You may not believe me, but it is very hard to stop using a credit card because you are forced to wait to buy something that you were in the habit of getting right when you wanted it, not when you could afford it. Eventually, a lot of us fall and become victims of our own bad habits, and I desperately do not want us to fall victim to credit card debt, no matter what our reason was for using the credit card in the first place.

To add more urgency to this issue, it may help to understand how much interest you are actually paying once you fall behind on a payment and start to make the "minimum payment." The annual percentage rate ("APR") is probably something you have seen before if you are a frequent credit card borrower. If you see a credit card commercial soon, look for it — it will flash at the very end of the commercial and probably be in the bottom right or left corner. Likewise, if you get a credit card agreement, APR is usually in the smallest print possible, but it has mega implications. Essentially, this is the rate you are paying in yearly equivalent interest on your unpaid credit card balance. Also keep in mind that the interest is compounded monthly. What this means is that the interest you do not pay back on your credit card each month has interest assessed on it. For example, take the following scenario where you owe $1,000 on your credit card bill at a monthly interest of 1%. You would owe $1,000 + $10 of interest at the end of the month. If you go another month without paying your initial bill, you will start with your old balance of $1,010 and owe interest of $10.10 on that balance for a balance of $1,020.10 at the end of the next month. That $1,020.10 includes interest that you were assessed last month, so in a sense, that $10 of initial interest (that you were not able to spend at the mall) is now also accruing interest.

This is the power of compounding and the way that credit card companies make a lot of their money. They are earning interest on interest that you owe, as well as earning interest on the loan you took out with them (the initial purchase you made that you have not yet paid back in full).

There are certainly going to be emergencies in life, and if a credit card is the last resort and you are confident that you will make the repayment immediately, that could be an exception to the rule. Please make those repayments immediately, rather than falling into the trap of just paying the minimum balance. It is always going to be more fun to pay the minimum balance, as the full balance is costly and could make you cut down on your lifestyle for a few months. As I mentioned earlier, in general, I don't like seeing people use credit cards because they create bad habits. It creates the habit of wanting something now and purchasing it with money you don't possess, instead of waiting until later (when you can afford it). I have heard from some people that they need to have a credit card and make regular purchases on it because they need to build their credit. A lender is not going to deny you a home loan because you refuse to use a credit card. If you came to a lender with a lot of money in savings, a stable job, and little or no debt, you will not have major issues getting a competitive loan. The goal of this book is for you to become more financially responsible and have a healthy personal balance sheet and income statement. Thus, if the situation calls for it, you will not have a problem getting a loan if you want to take out some "good debt."

Second on our list of bad debt is car loan debt. A good rule of thumb is that if you can't buy the car right now, you probably don't need to be driving it. Another thing to remember is that a car isn't a traditional financial asset. A car's value declines significantly once you drive it off the lot, and it will continue to depreciate from then on until you sell it. Do not expect to receive positive cash flow from a car during the time you own it. You will not receive dividends or a check in the mail every month thanking you for buying the car. You will instead pay for:

- Insurance;
- Taxes;
- Gas; and
- Maintenance.

If you critically evaluate your car and the lack of cash inflows from it versus the numerous cash outflows, it is essentially just a glorified personal expense. I have no problem putting a car on a personal balance sheet, but I certainly would consider it to be a much lower quality asset when compared to cash, investments or an equity stake in a business. As such, I put a car loan in the same bucket as using a credit card for designer suits or that amazing "something" that you don't need. Of course, not taking out a car loan could mean you drive a car that isn't as nice as your friends (who lease or borrowed), but you will have the financial freedom to put those car payments to better use. How can I say this? Well, as I am writing this book, I still drive a 1995 Toyota Avalon that makes the most bizarre noises on the road. In addition, this car has severe body damage courtesy of another Atlanta driver. But it gets the job done, and I don't have any car payments to make each month. There is no stress in the Giuliani household when it comes to cars, and we like it that way. One day we will replace this car for something else that we can afford to pay for with cash.

It is amazing how much more money we would have if we viewed our car as a mode of transportation rather than an expression of ourselves (e.g., current status), and if we did not need to have all the upgrades on our car for it to be an "acceptable" vehicle.

I am not advocating that you get a car that is ultra-cheap and causes you to be in danger or a car that is ultra-unreliable. Rather, I want you to develop a certain mentality — a mentality that allows you to look at a car with sober judgment, so that the purchase of a car does not end up causing you to suffer financially in the near and long term.

Our current Honda Accord at one time had a car loan tied to it (not my decision). The payment was approximately $500 a month and I cringed every time we wrote that check. The last payment we made on that car was incredible. An overwhelming wave of relief washed over me as I realized there would be no more debt payments — we had finally been released from the chains of our car debt. This fully paid car was now ours. Immediately after that memorable day, we were able to create amazing savings momentum. My wife and I both view this as one of the key turning points in our journey to financial security. This will be the last auto loan we ever get, and that is not just because of our current financial position. It is a mentality we have developed. There are exceptions to everything, but if one is in need of a car, it is my belief that focused saving can get a person to a place where they can get an acceptable car to meet their daily needs. You may need to take public transportation for a while or think of other creative ways to get to work, but I believe eventually you can all buy a car, loan free, if you hold to a straight and narrow path of financial discipline.

One last example of bad debt is any type of loan where you pledge your equity earned in an investment as collateral to receive a loan, such as a business venture or the equity on your current house or rental properties. If you are like me and bought a house in 2007, you are probably thinking, "People actually can have equity in their house?" Amazingly, the answer is yes, as there are still houses that have a nice cushion between the home's appraised value and the mortgage balance tied to the house. Generally speaking, pledging equity as collateral should be avoided at all costs. The financial emergency (significant medical bills, etc.) is of course the ultimate exception to most rules, but if you exclude the harshest of circumstances, an equity collateral type loan can easily be abused and tied to purchases that are rooted in a desire to have something now, rather than when you can actually afford to make the purchase. I am in total agreement that a new tile splash in the kitchen or the addition of a steam feature to your shower would be unbelievable, but do you need to borrow to do it? New appliances would be great, but is it really the right time to purchase them if you need to borrow against your equity to do so?

With lending restrictions tightening after the recent loan crisis, equity collateral type loans of any nature will become harder to attain and could require a time consuming application process. This is a good prevention control for you because you should be avoiding this type of debt. In today's environment, if you have equity in your house or your business, count yourself blessed. This equity position in your house gives you the advantage of being able to more easily move from your house should you want to live somewhere else. If you have equity in a business, this could be to your advantage should you desire to sell it. You could also use your retained earnings to fund your retirement or reinvest into your business. There are a lot of people that are trapped in their houses because they owe more on their house than it is worth. Do not compromise that advantage by putting yourself into more housing debt.

Managing Your Debt

Now that you understand debt, good or bad, how do you manage it? Like most things of a financial nature, it is always advisable to start with a well thought out plan. I like to list my debt in order of payment priority. The interest rate on your debt is the most important criteria to consider when you decide which debt you would like to extinguish first. If you have credit card debt, this will likely be the debt with your highest interest rate, and it should be attacked as soon as possible. It would be ideal to make more than the minimum payment when trying to pay down your credit card balance (if at all possible, pay the outstanding balance in one payment). Simply stated, credit card balances are not good, and you do not want this to be a long-term loan. Lastly, credit card interest is not tax deductible. The combination of high interest and no tax benefit makes this a bad debt, and one that you will want to pay down quickly.

Typically, next in order of interest rate debt will be your mortgage. For a period of time, you may need to make the minimum payments on this debt. However, if this debt becomes the highest interest loan on your personal balance sheet, paying more than the minimum balance is worth considering.

Every extra dollar you pay above the minimum balance on your mortgage decreases the amount of interest that you will pay in the future.

If you have time, look up a mortgage payment schedule calculator on the internet. You will quickly notice that a lot of what you pay over the life of your mortgage is interest. Your total interest payment over the life of a loan is going to be a function of the size of your debt balance, the length of the loan and your stated rate. If you always make the minimum payment, you will pay the maximum amount of interest. If you make more than the minimum payment, you will pay less than the maximum amount of interest, and will save yourself in interest payments. This rule should be balanced with a well thought out view of your other investment opportunities. If you have $100 available for investment and you want to take the risk trying to make 10% in another investment, it could make sense to use that $100 for that investment, rather than saving yourself future interest payments at a 5% rate by paying down your debt early. This is entirely a function of your appetite for risk and whether the risk return tradeoff on the 10% investment makes sense.

While on the topic of mortgages, it is very important to understand the current interest rate environment. Currently, mortgage rates are at historical lows. This provides the opportunity for those of you that have older mortgages to refinance. Refinancing is a great way to manage debt because it is essentially trading your current debt for debt with better terms (lower interest). Typically, there are closing costs associated with refinancing, so you will want to consider those costs when refinancing, as these closing costs can be pretty substantial. If you think you will be in a house for a while, you will usually cover these closing costs after a period of time because refinancing will allow you to make lower monthly payments on your mortgage. The lower payments you get through refinancing really bring to light the impact of a lower interest rate on the calculation of your required monthly minimum mortgage payment. Your home will need to be appraised before you can refinance. If your house's market value is significantly lower than the current balance on your loan, you may not be approved for a refinancing arrangement, or you may need to pay an interest rate very similar to your current rate. Refinancing can be a useful tool when managing your debt because you can see immediate benefits through enjoying lower debt payments each month, allowing you to pay off your debt faster than you would otherwise, and providing you with more cash to meet your daily needs if your current debt balance was making it hard to get from paycheck to paycheck.

Hopefully it is clear how important it is to have a logical battle plan when attempting to manage your debt. In an ideal world there would be no debt. But unfortunately life does not always work that way, and there are things you want to accomplish and dreams you want to chase that could require the use of debt for a season of your life. A major key to your financial success is whether you are going to avoid the bad debt and manage the good debt responsibly, with the hope that this debt served its purpose for a season of your life and is eventually paid in full.

Charity Principles

The theme of charity has already appeared a few times in this book, with the primary focus being on what it can do for us from a tax perspective. But what if you take the focus off of yourself for a second and think about the act of giving without ever receiving a tangible monetary benefit in return? In my experience, the reward in giving is the feeling that you made someone else better off as a result of your generosity. There isn't a dollar value you can place on that feeling. To believe this principle on faith is risky, but the rewards are priceless; it is such a great feeling that to try and make it equivalent to something you would buy with money would be unwise. I have a deep passion for using the power of money to help the common good. It is no secret that money is the easiest way for us to transact. Using money is so ingrained in most of us that it is hard to imagine surviving without money. As you can probably tell, you can make a big difference in the lives of others by using your money responsibly.

Charitable giving is a difficult concept. Do I personally give money to every person who asks for it? No. Have there been people that have used money I have given them to go buy liquor or drugs? Possibly. Should those people to whom I gave money try to get a job? Maybe. Here is the point: I am very passionate about developing the right heart and a healthy view toward money. How amazing would this world be if money meant so much more than what it can do for us in this lifetime? Many of the readers of this book give to some cause, and I think that is fantastic. To me it is very interesting that the Bible often references poverty. Interestingly, in Leviticus 25:35 (New International Version) it says:

"If an Israelite becomes poor and cannot support himself, help him."

In today's environment, you can assume that this verse is talking about both genders and all races of people. Also interesting is that the verse does not distinguish between degrees of poor people. It doesn't infer that one should help the poor person who worked hard and recently lost his or her job, but not help the person who has done drugs and lives on the streets. Conversely, if you gave all your money away, how would you take care of yourself? Someone would then have to give you money to survive. This is truly a difficult concept and one that I personally struggle to consistently follow. I don't give to every poor person who asks for it, but can I do more than I do now? When I drive and see a man or woman with a sign, do I drive by, even though I have spare cash or food in the car? Do I put my head down and act like I don't notice them? Do you?

Give your money and get something better in return:

I know from personal experience that giving to others has an interesting way of coming back to you in ways you don't even expect. During prayer, it will occasionally be on my heart to thank Jesus for the financial setbacks that I did not experience that day: things like avoiding a costly flat tire when I run into another hidden Atlanta pothole or not having my car break down randomly on the road. If you have seen my car, you know that having it not breaking down is proof that prayer works. In a sense, this is just as good as having a sudden windfall of cash rain down from the sky. The point of giving is not to expect something good in return, but rather the good thing in return is the feeling that you made a difference, that your hard work met your needs and then the extra you had went to making someone else's life a little easier.

Luke 11:41 (New International Version) says it this way:

"But now as for what is inside you—be generous to the poor, and everything will be clean for you."

It is interesting that this verse touches on two very important concepts. The first is our treatment of the poor, and the second is the impact on our inside (or our heart) when we are generous to the poor. How many times are we generous to the poor? Jesus did not say to give the pennies in your ashtray or your worst things to the poor, but rather to give generously. Merriam-Webster.com defines "generous" as liberal in giving, or open handed. This is a very tough standard, and if you just think about your money and how hard you worked for it, it is very easy to dismiss this request from Jesus as being too hard. If I have $20 in my wallet, and I see someone in need, my first thought could be, "$20 is too much money to give. I wish I had some ones." Am I being open handed in that situation? No, and I want to continually improve in this area. I encourage you to take on this challenge with me.

"But what is the point?" someone may ask. It is my money, I worked for it, and I deserve to use it! Jesus anticipated that question when he made the initial statement about giving to the poor: "…and everything will be clean for you"(New International Version). Clean does not mean financially clean in this context. The verse is talking about what is inside of us. Money is a huge heart issue for many of us. How many of us constantly think about our money, worry about it, strive for it? That mentality may have even been what led you to buy this book. Since Jesus was fully man and experienced everything humans feel and face, I also think Jesus understands how important money may be to us. And how could we not make it a priority? Growing up in the 20th century and now living in the 21st, I cannot even imagine a society where money is not the medium of exchange. More than anything, Jesus knows that if we are willing to lay down the things that we want for ourselves and shift those resources to someone who is so poor that they cannot even meet their basic needs like food and shelter, we are on the path to becoming "clean on the inside." People that are clean on the inside and have this healthy view toward money don't create Ponzi schemes or make company decisions that only benefit themselves and hurt the employees and shareholders of the company. They don't make the selfish decisions that cause recessions and depressions and all the economic issues that have left many in a tough financial spot. On a more relatable scale, maybe with people more clean on the inside, we won't see people brought to financial ruin by an inability to control their vices. If you are truly honest with yourself, I think you would appreciate being able to have more trust in the financial system, whether you believe Jesus' words or not.

We can't all change the world by ourselves. We certainly can't afford to bankroll every poor person or give to everyone who asks for our assistance. Still, I think many of us never achieve financial peace because we are living too closed-handed with our finances. We are deceived by the thought that financial peace comes through having a certain amount of money. I have found much more joy in being able to succeed financially and share that money with others. You can really brighten someone's day by buying them an unexpected lunch. I have found that there is peace in knowing that your daily needs are met. I want you all to plan for your financial future and to give you the tools to do so. At the same time, when you get to your financial goals, I want you to enjoy being there, rather than living with discontentment. One way I have witnessed the evaporation of financial discontentment is through generosity in prosperity. I think we all go through a stage where we need to think a lot about ourselves. We need to get to a certain financial level before we can even think about others. I can hear someone say, this book is supposed to be about me becoming financially secure, so how can I do that if I am giving it away? I can answer that for you: I want you to become financially secure, enjoy that financial security and be loved by others. You won't have all three of these things if you hold your finances with a tight fist.

How You Can Give

As touched on earlier in the tax principles section of this book, donations to charitable organizations are generally tax deductible. Thus cash contributions to charities are a very common practice, and are generally the easiest way to give. I think you can find a cause worth giving cash to on a regular basis. A lot of organizations have made the giving process very easy and secure, mainly through web donation options.

Though cash is the cleanest way to give, donation of other financial assets, such as stocks, can be useful to charities and provide a tax benefit. When you donate a stock to a charity it receives a step up in basis, which means that the charity records the stock at the current market value and you generally get a tax deduction equal to the current market value of the stock. A charity is then able to sell the stock without incurring tax, and can use the proceeds to help fund the operations of the charity.

For the more affluent, a foundation is a very efficient way to tax plan and have a positive impact on one or multiple charities. The foundation can be very expensive to start and maintain, so it is not a very common vehicle for charitable giving purposes. A foundation is unique in that it's a charity in itself that you contribute to, which then makes contributions to charities of your choosing. You can use a foundation as a way to lower your estate taxes, especially if a lot of your wealth is tied up in non-cash assets with a low cost basis and high current market value. By contributing these non-cash assets to the foundation, an individual is able to get a tax deduction off the current market value of the contributed assets and then the foundation is able to sell the non-cash assets, free of tax, for later distribution to a charity of choice.

An alternative way to give to charity is via the donor advised fund. These are more feasible for those people that are not incredibly wealthy. Donor advised funds are very useful tools for individuals that want to give to a certain cause, but do not want to start a foundation. A donor advised fund allows one to donate stock to a fund complex, and take a tax deduction for the market value at the date the stock is gifted. The unrealized appreciation on the stock is not taxable to the donor advised fund (the increase in the value of the stock from the day you purchase it to the date that you donate it), and any increases in the value of the stock while it is in the fund are also not taxed. This is a much better option than the scenario where someone has some stock and they sell it, get taxed on the gain and then donate the cash to the charity. This is growing in popularity and is worth communicating to a financial professional if you feel led to donate in this manner. A financial professional should be able to locate a few possible options for you, saving you from the risk of donating to a fund that the IRS does not recognize as charitable for tax purposes.

Hopefully I have accomplished our two goals for this chapter: to impress upon you the importance of giving, and to provide you with some financially savvy ways to give to others. Personally I enjoy giving in a controlled manner, whereby I have some assurance that the money I am donating is going directly to the cause I support. The biggest hurdle is going to be letting go of the furious cling to our money; I fight it too sometimes. It is so easy to procrastinate when the topic of giving comes up. Money can buy a lot of things, but it can't buy the intrinsic peace and satisfaction of selflessly giving to those in need.

Patience, Timing, and Delayed Gratification Principles

This will be a tough section for most, because it is the one area of your finances that you cannot defer to someone else. You can hire professionals to handle your taxes, investments, or retirement goal range, but you cannot hire someone to prevent you from spending your own money. In this chapter, I introduce the idea of "delaying gratification," which requires you to challenge the urge to reward yourself and to say "I deserve it" when you are faced with the temptation to buy something that is a bit of a stretch for you (or requires some of that "bad debt"). Some will immediately think this is ridiculous. Here in the U.S., I am free to spend on anything I want, and if my bank account says I have enough money, then who is going to stop me? Savings account? What is that? I want these shoes, and they match that new top I just bought earlier in the day. This may seem like a bit of an exaggeration, but clamping down on our spending is so hard, right? Money is an unbelievable concept. Who can tame it?

A lot of our society is misled by the illusion that if they get just a bit more, they will have all that they will ever need.

Before I get accused of being disconnected from modern society, let me say that I totally understand how a lot of you feel. You work hard, you set goals, and at some point you get close enough to the things you want in life. Even though it may not be "your time," you want it to be your time, and you take action. Maybe for some of you it is a car. Or maybe for some it's a house or a vacation property. It can even be the little things you buy that, when added together, really make up a good portion of your spending. Because a car purchase is a common illustration of where people are susceptible to not having patience, not demonstrating the appropriate financial timing, and ultimately not delaying gratification, it will be the primary discussion point for the majority of this chapter. If you don't connect to the car example, it should be easy to plug in another material possession that could make you susceptible to the temptation of purchasing an item when you aren't in the right financial position to do so.

I am not going to tell you that you don't need a car. In lieu of an amazing public transportation system (like in New York City), it is a pretty big necessity in a developed country like the United States. However, you do need to do things like challenge what kind of car you really need and can afford.

It is recommended to avoid buying a car that has payments greater than 10% of your gross annual income.

First of all, it is not just the cost of the car. It is also the interest you pay on the car loan if you choose to borrow. (This interest is not tax deductible and thus is considered "bad interest.") There are also ad valorem costs that can be very high with a nicer car. Ad valorem taxes are paid on the value of the car (value-added tax). There is the hike in insurance you pay on a more expensive car, another expenditure that is neither an investment in your future nor tax deductible. Have you considered the more expensive cost for service if you need to have repairs?

I'm a car guy myself. I would be lying if I said I have never dreamed of owning a Ferrari, or that I didn't enjoy the time on my honeymoon where we got to drive a Mercedes SL500 for one day. For me, though, there are so many more important things than how cool I look or what people think about me having a certain type of car. (Both of these things should not matter to any of us by the way.) Even if having a car like this has nothing to do with appearance, it has so many opportunity costs. Does that mean I think people shouldn't buy it, even if they can afford it? Not necessarily. If a very nice car is a miniscule part of your income, and you have no financial burden making insurance, tax and repair payments on the car, go for it and count yourself very blessed. If someone has no problem affording a car, they should be free to buy whatever car they want. What I want to challenge you to think about is whether you can actually afford the car.

One indicator for knowing whether you can truly afford a car is whether you can pay cash for it on the date of purchase.

I juxtapose this against the situation where you can only afford a certain car if you eat noodles each night and even then can just barely make the minimum payments due on the car. These are two entirely different life scenarios and are a good barometer for determining whether you have a set of wheels that is above what you can afford. In general, I am a huge proponent of paying cash for a car. Generally, when you use cash to purchase a car, it would be in a non-distressed situation. Borrowing to buy a car is usually a signal to me that you are not entirely ready to make a car purchase. If a life emergency happens and you absolutely need a car and are low on cash, I would just challenge you to get the minimum car that meets your needs.

On my 1995 Toyota Avalon, I pay about $30 a year in taxes. My Toyota Avalon is almost at the point where my tag fees every year exceed the tax on my car. Insurance is also low, and it has been a truly reliable car. Repairs have been very minimal, and I am so grateful about how well this car has handled a tough Atlanta driving environment. I know what you may be thinking: "I don't want to drive an old car." And I get that. I think the major point here is that a car is designed to get you around, not cause financial stress or require living paycheck to paycheck.

Leasing a Car vs. Purchasing a Car

Some people, in their aim to get in the nicest car possible, will go the leasing route. Leasing a car is attractive for the individual that cannot secure a loan on a car or likes the idea of trading in their car every few years for something better. It is very important to check the terms of the lease agreement as it can be very easy to unintentionally violate some of the lease rules. For example, if you drive the car too many miles during the lease term you could end up paying more money on your lease than you expected. It's important to be very careful of falling into the trap of using a lease as a way to get into a car that you really want but can't afford at the moment. There are exceptions to this lease rule, so the final word of caution on leasing a car is to determine your motivation for getting the lease. I would not lease just because you want to drive an expensive car that you cannot afford to pay with cash. I recommend going with a car that is within your means and that you can preferably pay for with cash. If there is absolutely no way around it, borrow to obtain, but with reasonable loan terms. Challenge yourself to determine whether you really need to use debt to buy a car before you sign the purchase agreement.

It Feels Like We Were Born to Want Stuff, and Want It Now

Saying no to things we want now is not natural for us at all. Try telling three-year-old kids that they cannot have what they want, the moment they want it. It is pretty much a set-up for a scream or waterworks festival. I can only imagine the look on a toddler's face if you were to tell her that it's not the right season or time for her to have a certain toy. However, this is exactly the mentality they need to develop, and the earlier the better. There are people that truly can buy anything they want, and it is not an issue for them. To those I would say, "Wow, you are blessed, and I pray that you change the world for the better with your blessed financial situation." For the rest of us, though, trying to get everything we want, when we want it, can and will put us in a financial bondage that is so much harder to get out of than it would be to avoid in the first place.

It takes a little faith, in my opinion, to believe in the importance of delaying gratification. However, I have found two amazing takeaways as a result of practicing this mentality. First of all, when you delay gratification and finally obtain what you were originally seeking, you will enjoy it more. Why? Mainly because you will appreciate the discipline involved in getting to the point where you could make the purchase, and also because you will not have the financial stress tied to the object, which would otherwise make it less enjoyable. Another amazing result of delaying gratification, and the one that I like the best, is that sometimes God will give you a renewed understanding of things, which will allow you to have the wisdom and foresight to challenge whether you need the thing at all. I think it is amazing when our hearts change and we start to see the beauty in giving rather than receiving. We will be so empty and disappointed at the end of our lives if we are just motivated by things and possessions. If we can stave off the thirst to buy something now, while it could cause us financial bondage, it allows time for our hearts to change and to instead position ourselves to be in a place where we can help others. The most difficult state to be in if you want to help someone out is financial bondage. It is so crippling, and it causes us to be so preoccupied with our own situation that we lose sight of other important things around us. How heartbreaking would it be to see someone in desperate need, but not be able to help them out because we either have no money or are too worried about how giving will impact our own financial situation. If we can delay gratification, I believe we will be in a better place financially, more easily able to buy the things we need and sometimes the things we don't need, but really want (sometimes we need little rewards in life), and we will be more able to see the needs of those around us.

Maybe for you cars aren't the big item. Maybe the thing you can't wait to buy is that dream house you have always wanted. It has custom rooms and is the type of house that you hire an architect to design. Or perhaps maybe it is just a bigger house, in the perfect neighborhood. Or maybe you just want a house, any house. You have been patient, the timing is not quite right, but someone showed you how you could get that house today, if you just "signed here." That someone of course is a mortgage broker and what you are signing is the obligation to pay off a sizable debt before that house is completely yours. If I were to speak to you personally right now, I would tell you to wait. A house is much different than a car. You likely aren't going to be able to pay cash for it, but that does not mean that you shouldn't exercise outstanding discipline when deciding on the right time to buy the right house.

In general, a mortgage or rent payment should not be 25% or more of your annual gross income.

If it exceeds that amount you are likely over extended and putting yourself in a spot where you could have a financial emergency if one thing doesn't go right. I want you to walk away from this book with the intent of delaying gratification so that when your toaster breaks or you get a flat tire, you don't have a major blow up or severe financial stress. In a sense, that is what this section is about: waiting until you can make purchases that do not represent large chunks of your income, do not put significant pressure on you, and do not add to your worry. I want you to be that person who does a marvelous job with their finances and is able to make a dream purchase. But mostly, I want you to get there in the right season, with the right personal balance sheet (assets greater than liabilities). You will always enjoy the fruits of your labor when they are enjoyed in the right season. Has anyone tried to eat a mango when it wasn't ripe? It's a pretty brutal experience. But when it is the right time and the right season, it can be fantastic fun! I think a house is the same way. Try to grab hold of it too early and you get in a house that has payments that are too high for you to maintain. You could end up having a beautiful house that is empty, because all you can afford is the housing payment and electric bill (unless of course you borrow to buy furniture as well). In a situation like this, you are almost forced to always think about money, preventing you from saving for other areas like retirement.

Gaining a Mature Perspective Trumps Merely Fighting the Urge to Spend Beyond Our Means

So what is it for you? I mentioned a car and a house, as these tend to be two of the bigger items that people struggle with when it comes to delaying gratification. For me personally, it's a table tennis table (don't call it ping pong please) that I have wanted for seven years. I currently live in a two bedroom condo and tried to sell my wife on the idea of us cramming a table tennis table and a table tennis robot into our living room. I measured it out and everything. As long as I don't step two feet to my left, I won't put a hole in the wall! My wife is too nice, and actually said she was okay with it. My table tennis purchase was starting to gain some serious momentum! I put a table tennis table in my "basket" and almost checked out when I had to stop myself from making the purchase. How can I write a chapter on delaying gratification when I am about to buy a championship table tennis table for my living room? I closed my webpage and looked forward to the day when a table tennis table would make its way into my abode. Someday I'll have that table, but it's not the right season of my life yet.

It is so important to understand the explicit and implicit costs of making a purchase that is not in the correct season of our life. Explicit costs are pretty easy to spot. Examples of explicit costs could be the payments you make each month on your car or on your mortgage. The implicit costs could be the increased stress or lost opportunity costs because you have committed to a large loan. Meeting financial goals you set for yourself can be very fulfilling, and rewarding yourself is an understandable desire. When you get that dream car, house, or whatever, my desire is for you to be positioned well enough financially to enjoy every day of owning it. This is so much better than having a big rush of initial excitement, only to be undone by the stress caused by the financial burden of owning an expensive house or car.

There are some things that I could want my whole life but that I may never attain. However, it is my hope that those things I want now will lose their luster as I gain more perspective, and I will learn to be content in all things. In fact, one of the prayers I frequently have is that God will give me the heart to love people and the wisdom to understand how to manage blessings in my life. I have found that the answer to that prayer is not necessarily God giving me a bunch of stuff and forcing me to be generous with it. In some areas of my life, He has changed my heart so that I do not prioritize possessions so much. My favorite teaching in the Bible regarding possessions is from Matthew 6:19-20:

"Do not store up for yourselves treasures on earth, where moths and vermin destroy, and where thieves break in and steal. But store up for yourselves treasures in heaven, where moths and vermin do not destroy, and where thieves do not break in and steal."

I do not think Jesus is saying that possessions are a bad thing to have or that you should feel guilty for wanting to have a new car. However, I think the advice here is that the pursuit of possessions should not become such a part of your life that you ruin your relationship with God and others. You can ruin the relationships with the most important people in your life when you are in so much debt or so stressed about anything happening to your stuff that you are no fun to be around. It is much easier, in my opinion, to wait one more year for that new car when the timing is right and when you begin to understand that possessions are fleeting and are not meant to rule over you.

To end this section, I leave you with the following quote by Winston Churchill, a quote that has changed the way I view the world and may be helpful to you as well:

"We make a living by what we get, but we make a life by what we give."

Savings Principles

When I hear people say, "Save your money," a lot of things come to mind. I have thoughts of bringing my lunch to work, crock pot meals designed to feed for days, or buying a 50 pound turkey at Thanksgiving so I can eat turkey sandwiches until well after Christmas. It is probably safe to assume that at one point you have tried to save money, but I would venture to guess that many of you save a lot less money than you initially planned. In this chapter, I will unveil the great secret to saving money. But to start, I will discuss why saving money is important in the first place.

Why Saving Is Important

First of all, saving money develops financial discipline. This is one of the key fundamentals to achieving financial success. When you save money, you retain rather than spend. You ensure that you have money for the right season or the right opportunity, the opportunity that you could not have seized had you been lacking available cash. This seems so simplistic, but why is it so difficult? The common answer I hear in practice is that people just have enough to meet their weekly expenses, and thus cannot save. I do not doubt this is true; however, what exactly are the weekly expenses? Are these weekly expenses things you can do without if your chief purpose is to attain financial success? I think this is the first question you need to honestly ask yourself if you are serious about saving money. It would be easy at this point to go on a rant about the things you buy that you don't need, but that isn't the focus of this chapter, and in truth, those are conversations you need to have with yourself. None of us are perfect spenders, so I don't intend to condemn here, but rather to challenge you to honestly evaluate your expenditures.

Where Is Your Money Going?

If you have no idea what you spend and where you spend it, then start tracking your expenditures today. Ultimately, it would be ideal for you to come up with a list of discretionary expenditures that you can challenge and subsequently remove as a spending habit. Make this list in writing rather than mentally. There is something permanent and striking about the written word. The expenditure that you are struggling with will look a lot more real to you when you see it on paper with the cost and the associated frequency. Think long and hard about the items that you buy frequently. Start eliminating the smaller expenditures (do you really need to chew a bucket of gum each day), and then if you get bold, make bigger expenditure elimination decisions. The key in all of this is to develop a financial discipline whereby you don't buy everything that you want, and you think critically about buying only what you need. The difference this will make on your financial outlook will be gratifying because it is immediate. When I decide not to buy the most expensive item on the menu at a restaurant, it is like someone sent me a check for $10 + tip and tax. When this idea starts to sink in fully, you will start to develop a financial habit whereby you almost feel bad about spending when you know it is not something you need. Currently, many fail at saving because they justify their spending; they have been so used to buying things whenever the thought pops in their head. The reason for your excessive expenditures is irrelevant, and I'm not going to list the items you need to challenge, but I think when you are serious enough about your financial success, you will think about the items you currently buy that are keeping you from saving effectively.

The Secret of Savings

Now that you have made the decision that you are going to be a disciplined saver, what do you do with your money? I think this is covered pretty well in the earlier parts of the book where I discuss pre-tax contributions to employer-sponsored defined contribution plans and/or personal investing. An extra benefit of making pre-tax contributions to a 401(k) plan is that it forces you to save before you get the opportunity to spend the money. As you now know, there is a dollar point where the 401(k) pre-tax contributions get maxed out. Thus, you will need to save money once it comes into your possession, rather than spending it frivolously. So how do you do it effectively?

The secret is pretty simple, almost too simple, but oh so effective. Do it now! Saving is not natural, so start small if it seems unnatural. This is an area that I turn over to God many times, asking him to put it on my heart to save so that He can do better things with my money than I would do on my own. So many are inclined to spend what they have, and procrastinate their savings decision to the "next pay check." Start now by picking a desired savings percentage of your periodic paycheck and gradually move the savings percentage upward over time. Avoid picking an incredibly high percentage to save each month, as there is the potential to fail horribly, get discouraged and then not save anything at all.

Whenever you are trying to establish new habits, you need to develop confidence. You need to see yourself succeeding in a small capacity, so that you have the will to continue on and allow time for the habit to anchor. I always recommend starting with something so small it would be inexcusable for me to miss.

A good starting point is 3%. Can you save 3%? Sure you can, and if you can't, you need to make a long list of items you spend your money on each week and email it to me so we can discuss what can be removed from your monthly spending. Notice, I did not say it would be easy to save 3%, but merely that I think you can do it if you truly desire. Week one your goal will be 3%. Week two your goal will be the same and your short-term goal is to get to week four, where you are still saving 3%. This would be an entire month of saving 3%, something that maybe you have never accomplished in your life, and definitely something to cheer about. Once you lock in that 3%, move it up to 3.1% on your next paycheck, and then 3.2% thereafter and so on. The 0.1% impact is usually a few dollars, but it has a huge impact on gaining "Savings Momentum." Here is a savings chart for illustrative purposes:

Period	Savings Percentage
Weeks 1 – 4	3.0%
Weeks 5- 8	3.1%
Weeks 9 – 12	3.2%

Of course you will not want to just stop at 3.2%, and after 12 weeks, you begin establishing a lifetime habit. After 12 weeks, you will have the confidence that you can save and may then decide you want to challenge yourself further and raise your savings percentage even higher. The habit of saving will have firmly set in.

One of the best ways to execute a savings rate is to take it off the top. Once you get paid, your 3% or whatever the figure is, should immediately be transferred from checking to savings, and not touched again. I find that it is so much easier to save the money at the beginning of the month when you have more money than closer to your next paycheck when you are running low and need the little extra to get through the week.

If you are like me, you would also want to know an exciting benefit of saving money. I think it is simple — opportunity. Imagine saving enough cash so that your significant other is able to take a less stressful job or no job at all? Another opportunity could be that business you always wanted to start, but never could because you didn't have the seed capital to make that initial investment. In fact, this book would not have been possible if I had not learned the importance of saving money, as it required some of my own savings to produce and market this publication. Maybe it is sending your child to the college they never would have been able to go to otherwise. Another option is being able to take advantage of an investment opportunity that you have researched and feel confident in pursuing. Finally, you could make that charitable contribution you always wanted to make, but never thought you could afford. These are just a couple of ideas. I encourage you to come up with your own exciting savings goals. Part of the excitement in saving is seeing the ultimate end goal of that saving.

It could also help to hear about my own personal savings success story. My wife and I used the method in this book and were able to gradually attain a large amount of cash savings. We bought a condo at the top of the market ($182,000), only to see it plummet in value once the economy crashed. Coinciding with this decrease in the housing market was the need for more space for our first son. At first, I thought we could put him in our room, but I think I was being too thrifty with that thinking. We decided in 2012 that we would finally move and aggressively try to sell our unit. We were frustrated by continually lowering our listing price to the point where it was half of what we paid for it.

Finally we got an offer; we got excited. We then found out the offer was for $85,000, almost $100,000 less than we paid for the unit four years previously. After a little negotiating, we got the amount to $88,750 only to find that no lender wanted to give our buyer a loan because we lived in an HOA community that was not FHA approved. The only way we could sell is if we negotiated a cash deal with the buyer. Eventually we agreed on a purchase price of $80,000, over $100,000 less than our purchase price. To make this sale we had to bring over $60,000 to the closing table. Can you imagine having to pay $60,000 to sell your house? Had we not followed the savings plan in this book we would still be in our one bedroom condo with no hope in sight. We were able to wire over $60,000 and still have a good portion of savings left over. This was not because we were extremely wealthy (though we are immensely blessed by our Lord), it was because we had the discipline for five years to put away cash when it would have been tempting to buy nice cars, have an expensive sports cable package, and do all kinds of shopping. Saving money is something I believe in because I know without the savings approach in this book, I would not have been able to give my family a better living situation. Saving money in this manner will work for anyone that is willing to give it a concerted effort. The rewards are not immediate, but they are totally worth it.

The Power of the Written Word

Lastly, if the following tips are not enough, I would go the final step and write down your savings goal. In practice, I have been most successful in reaching goals when I define the goal in writing and the date I expect to complete the goal. I encourage you to write your savings goal on an index card and look at it weekly.

A well thought, and frequently revisited goal, keeps us going when it is tempting to buy now rather than defer until tomorrow.

For example, your note card could have a goal of saving 3% of your income by 12/31/XX. Be aware of your own personal perils and have a battle plan to attack these hurdles. Perhaps a hurdle is that you watch infomercials late at night and get intrigued by these "glamorous products." Maybe you have a knack for making that impulse buy every time you wait in line at the grocery store. Write these pitfalls down and then think of ways to avoid your common spending pitfalls. If you need to look at your feet while you are line, and that is what keeps you from buying the bucket of gum, go for it. Whatever you decide, having a plan for saving your money is the best launching point to being a successful saver. Do not confuse this with "wishing" you were better at saving money.

The "Safety Reserve"

A key component of saving is what is called the "safety reserve." The safety reserve can be thought of as the money you have stashed away for when life throws us the proverbial curveball. If you have lived long enough, you have no doubt had a bad experience that you did not see coming - an event so random that you would never have been able to save for it in advance. This is why the safety reserve is such a key concept. It is an account you set up that acknowledges that a job layoff, natural disaster, health problem, or other unexpected income impact can occur at any time. We certainly never expect these events to happen or wish for them to happen, but having the extra money to handle the financial consequences relieves a lot of the stress. If you are a two income family, saving three months of paychecks should be sufficient. If you are a one income family, saving six months of paychecks in the safety reserve would be advisable. This cash should not be touched. It is also the first portion of savings you should fill up (even before funding your 401(k) plan).

You will likely have various savings goals. This could be saving for retirement, college, or a charitable cause. All of these are worthy savings goals, but the safety reserve should always take precedence, because it's a first line of defense if your income suddenly dries up. I think it is also helpful to develop rules for the safety reserve. You need to be very deliberate when spending this money. Ideally, it should be saved for spending money on housing, food, transportation, and any other absolute necessity that applies to your situation when in dire need. A poor use of the money in your safety reserve would be if you don't have enough money for wild king salmon and are not in the mood to settle for trout. Usually if you need to think about whether something would be smart for you to purchase, you should probably not be using your safety reserve to make those purchases.

Savings Vehicles

To close out this section on saving, it would be helpful to discuss the various savings vehicles available and when they would make sense for us. The safety reserve should be in a highly accessible savings vehicle. Most likely this will be a standard savings account or a certificate of deposit "CD" that is not long term in nature (six months or less). With a safety reserve the goal isn't about earning a large return on your investment, it is about ensuring that the money is available when you need it.

Another important savings goal for most is education. A 529 plan is a very beneficial savings vehicle for educational funding purposes. These nifty vehicles can be in either your name or a defined beneficiary (most likely a child). Any contribution you make to these plans will earn interest, and that interest will not be taxable on your federal income tax return, as long as you spend it for educational purposes in the future. Some 529 plans are also exempt from state tax, depending on the state you reside in.

Earlier, I covered the benefit of saving for retirement with a 401(k) plan and will not spend a lot of time on it now. Just remember that 401(k) plan has a tremendous benefit in that contributions grow tax-free and contributions are excluded from taxable income in the year you deposit. If you use a "Roth" option, you still have a tremendous savings benefit but it works a bit differently. A Roth 401(k) plan would require your contributions today to be included in your taxable income on the current year tax return. However, your earnings grow tax-free and when you receive your money at retirement, it is not taxable to you.

Saving for medical costs in the future is becoming more of a necessity than ever before. Gone are the days when you stay with a company your whole life and they pay for your medical expenses. On top of that, medical premiums are skyrocketing, and thus you need a plan to account for this potentially significant expense. An efficient savings solution is now available in the form of a HSA. It has an excellent triple tax benefit in that payroll contributions are excluded from your current year taxable income, the account grows tax-free, and any withdrawals you make for qualified health expenses are tax-free. Another great benefit is that these plans are portable, so you can start early in saving for health expenses in retirement without the fear of losing your account if you move to another company. In a related vein, the balance does not expire and there is no minimum expenditure that needs to be made each year to keep your HSA balance in good standing. It is important to note that there are annual contribution limits that vary by year and depend on your age. Ensure you are aware of these limits prior to making your contributions. Below is a table that summarizes the contribution limits for both 2012 and 2013:

Year	Individual	Family
2012	$3,100	$6,250
2013	$3,250	$6,450

This contribution limit also includes contributions made by employers. Also, once you reach age 55 you can make up "catch-up" contributions ($1,000 in 2012 and 2013). A lot of companies have been moving to high deductible health care plans with an HSA and will make a contribution to your account either every pay period or annually. Typically this money is yours to keep, and there is not a service requirement tied to it. You can't contribute to or open a HSA unless you participate in a high deductible plan. If you later move to a non-high deductible plan, you can use the funds in your HSA to pay for qualified health care expenses (not personal items), but you can no longer contribute to your HSA. The contributions made by your employer are not taxable to you. If you participate in health screenings or other preventive health care activities, some employers will fund your HSA with money for your medical expenses. This money is also tax-free. Read the HR or benefits section of your employer's website to ensure you are getting the maximum HSA benefit.

In summary, once you make the decision to start saving money consider these savings vehicles:

- Interest earning savings accounts or CDs;
- 529 Plans;
- Traditional 401(k), Roth 401(k), or other company sponsored defined contribution plans; and
- HSA

Budgeting Principles

"This year we are going on a budget." We have all said it or heard it, but how many of us have done it or seen it done successfully? Can we even define a budget? Why is this so hard for us? Why is it often a New Year's resolution that gets forgotten about in February? It is my opinion that at the core of budgeting successfully, is the following mentality: "I will have a plan for every dollar I earn." You can't be serious, right? I am dead serious. I realize this is a pretty intense outlook, but I can attest that it is effective nonetheless. Secondly, you need a budgeting framework you can easily implement. I think there are individuals out there with good intentions of getting on a budget that feel helpless because they do not have the tools to succeed. I am going to focus on the second item, because I am going to assume that if you picked up this book and have made it this far that you have both the discipline and the desire to effectively budget. If you don't, hopefully the following framework will be so simple and exciting that you will find yourself actively engaged in the art of budgeting.

The Perfect Budgeting Framework

The perfect budgeting framework is going to depend on everyone's unique needs and circumstances, but there are a couple of commonalities that we all share. I like to think of budgeting as having different buckets of money or different checkbooks for different spending needs. For example, we all have certain recurring expenses, such as utilities, insurance, cable bill, and other debt we need to address, etc. We also have a housing bill, whether it is mortgage or rent. Thus, without too much thought, we have two checkbooks we can set up. I will call them the recurring expense and housing "funds" or "buckets." I personally use "fund" in my own budgeting, but whatever term you want to use is fine. The key point is that you should set up two different accounts to track these expenses and the money allocated to pay these expenses. I also like to set up a recurring expense schedule that lists who I owe money to, in what pay period

I owe it, and approximately how much I owe. The following sections describe the different kinds of funds your budget may have.

Recurring Expenses and Housing Funds

The amount you put in both the recurring expenses and housing funds should be pretty well defined. If you know that your housing bill is $1,000 a month, you should put $500 in the housing fund each paycheck (assumes you get two paychecks a month). The recurring expense fund will have more variability than the housing fund, as things like utilities or cell phone bills can fluctuate each month based on usage. When you initially set up your budget, you should estimate these expenses based on experience, and allocate that amount of money to your recurring expense fund each paycheck. For example, assume you have an average utility bill of $100, a cell phone bill of $100, a student loan of $100, and a cable bill of $60. Further, the utility and cell phone bills are due at the end of the month and the student loan and cable bill are due in the middle of the month. In this case, you can allocate $200 to the recurring expense fund at the end of the month and also allocate $160 to the recurring expense fund in the middle of the month. The key point here is that you are allocating the projected amount of money each paycheck to meet these expenses, so you will need to make slight adjustments each month if your actual bills are slightly higher or lower than estimated, as can be the case with cell phone and utility bills.

Savings Fund

No financial plan or budget would be complete without an allocation to savings. Setting up a savings fund within your budget can help provide you the discipline to reach your savings goals. You should contribute to the savings fund every paycheck, and it should represent a percentage of each paycheck. It's helpful to come up with an attainable savings rate first, and then once you start saving, it's important not to drop down below this initial value. It is admirable to be optimistic and come out with a huge starting percentage to allocate to savings. However, it does not help to be overly aggressive with a savings percentage, continually miss it, and then lose faith in your ability to budget. I have found success by starting with a percentage I know I can attain and then gradually increasing it each paycheck (a very small increase such as .1%) until you reach a reasonable savings cap. By selecting a very small increase in your savings percentage each paycheck, you will be improving your saving ability in a very subtle manner, such that you may not even notice you are saving more. Your ten paycheck savings plan could start at 3% and go up to 4% over the ten paycheck periods. You may find once you get to 4% that you want to keep going to 4.1% and onward!

So pick your percentage, multiply it by your paycheck and then stash that money in your savings fund. Do not touch this money. You also should probably transfer the money to a savings account that pays higher interest than your checking account. This could be a CD, which gives you higher interest rates than standard checking accounts. The trade-off with a CD account is that you are not able to take the money out of the CD until the CD period is over. CDs can range from six months to five years. If you are going to use a CD, I would favor using the six month option as opposed to a longer period. A six month CD will keep you from having your money locked up for an extended period of time. Having flexibility with your finances is crucial in case of an emergency, so being able to know you have immediate access to your savings is a nice feeling. You can always enter another six month CD after six months if you do not have anywhere else to put your savings.

The idea is that you are paying yourself first by saving this money and not waiting until the end of the month when you have already spent most of your money and don't have enough to stash in a savings fund. If you wait until the end of the month to put money in savings, you will find that most of the time there is nothing left to save! It is so much easier to stash away money immediately when you get your paycheck, rather than waiting until you get through two weeks of living. In those two weeks, your mind will think of countless ways to spend that money that would otherwise go into savings. Personally, I don't trust myself, so I save first and spend later.

The savings fund is a necessity for every budget, no matter your individual circumstances. It is also important to note that contributions to a 401(k) plan count for your savings fund. Since these contributions are pre-tax (automatically made before you get your actual paycheck), you should add back those contributions to the base amount you use for allocating amounts to your budget. For example, if your paycheck is $2,000 and you contributed $100 to your 401(k) plan, you would want to use $2,100 as the basis for making your allocations to the rest of the funds in your budget. At least some of your contribution to the savings fund should be in cash instead of making all your contributions to your 401(k) plan or other type of investment vehicle. Doing this will allow you to have extra cash on hand in case of an emergency, take advantage of a unique investment opportunity, or possibly even save for a house. I like to call this the emergency fund portion of the savings fund. As mentioned in the savings chapter, an emergency fund should typically be equal to six months of paychecks for a household with one person on an active payroll or three months of paychecks if a household has two or more people on an active payroll. Make sure to fill this portion of the savings fund up first. Once you fill it up, you can focus on your investment and retirement savings, both of which are within the scope of the savings fund.

Giving Fund

We have covered our major bills, made an effort to budget for savings and now have room for one of my favorite things to spend on, giving. I call it the giving fund, but it can be the charity fund or whatever else you want to call it. It is a badge of honor to be responsible stewards of our wealth. We all have something we can contribute, and the amount does not matter as much as our heart to give toward a good cause. We all know deep down in our heart what we are really capable of giving and what amount would put us in financial crises. The message of this book is not to give all your money away to everyone in the world that needs it. We cannot solve the poverty problem alone, but each of us can make a difference. I am reminded of a powerful story (anonymous) I heard a while back and I paraphrase for you below, as the story is not my own, but based on my recollection of it:

A kid was on the beach throwing starfish that had washed ashore, outside of their natural, water filled environment. There were hundreds of starfish all along the coastline. For one kid to put all these starfish back into the ocean would have been impossible. One by one the kid methodically tossed starfish back into the ocean when he was approached by an older gentleman. The older gentleman remarked, "Kid, why are you doing this? You are never going to make a difference out here. Look at how many starfish there are, and as you throw one back in, two more come back to the shore." The kid threw a starfish back in the ocean and replied "I made a difference in that starfish's life."

That story has always stuck with me. It is so powerful. Should our lack of resources keep us from trying to make an impact, even if our contribution alone will not solve the problem of poverty? Sometimes I think we miss the opportunities to make a difference because we doubt we can, or we think our resources are too limited. I have always been amazed at what God can do with the miniscule amount of resources I give Him. If we can become percentage givers by setting a percentage of our budgets to a charitable purpose, two things will happen:

- First you will be amazed at how great you feel. The generosity and love it requires to give your hard earned resources to someone in need will reciprocate back to you. Often, you will not see a financial return for your giving, but the love that will come back to you based on your act of love is worth so much more than dollars. No budget is big enough to quantify the possession of love and peace in your heart after living a season or a life of faithful giving.

- Secondly, you will be amazed at how God can help you live on the remaining money in your budget, almost as if you never gave any away. If you allocate 10% of your budget to giving, God will make that other 90% act like 100%. It seems counterintuitive and it takes faith, but I have seen it happen in my own life and I believe it. For the person that does not believe in God or has questions about giving, be open-minded and give this a shot. You will be amazed at the results. I am aware of many generous people who are not believers in God that would be able to attest to the great feeling they get when they help someone financially, and further, how in their generosity they still found that they had enough to meet their needs.

Similar to the savings fund, the giving fund should be funded before you make your other monthly purchases. Why is that? For the same reason you fund your savings fund up front: it is a lot easier to give money to someone when you have your full paycheck versus when you only have some of your paycheck left at the end of a pay period. As a Christian, I believe in the importance of giving to the local Church, and thus that goes into my giving fund calculation. Before I learned how to budget, it would be so much harder to make the contribution to my local Church, and many times I fell short because it was so much easier to rationalize my need to buy something versus giving it to God. If you don't attend Church or believe in contributing to the Church, I would encourage you to find some cause that you do believe in and that is totally dependent on outside donations. There are countless examples of non-profit organizations that would not continue if not for the love and generosity of their donors. Start with a percentage you know you can contribute consistently, and commit to it going forward. Non-profit organizations have expense budgets and revenue projections and it helps a non-profit tremendously if they know they can count on you to make a consistent contribution. More importantly, though, you will feel like you are making a true difference by seeing yourself consistently giving money to a cause that can only operate on your generosity and the generosity of others.

One final thought on giving comes from a very special verse of the Bible from Mark 12:41-44 (New International Version):

"Jesus sat down opposite the place where the offerings were put and watched the crowd putting their money into the temple treasury. Many rich people threw in large amounts. But a poor widow came and put in two very small copper coins, worth only a few cents. Calling his disciples to him, Jesus said, 'Truly I tell you, this poor widow has put more into the treasury than all the others. They all gave out of their wealth; but she, out of her poverty, put in everything—all she had to live on.'"

I bring this up to help you challenge how much you decide to allocate to your giving fund. I think you know deep in your heart how much you have to offer for the betterment of others. There are truly some people that can only give 0.1% of their incomes, or otherwise risk financial ruin. I would applaud that person if they gave that 0.1% because even in the worst financial situation of their life, they thought about an amount that they could give to someone else. The Bible passage above gives a glimpse into how God views us and our money. He is more interested in your heart and willingness to give, than in how much you give. God does not need our money — He can make anything happen in this world without money, but He is after our heart. For those who don't believe in that, it does not take you off the hook. I think most of us deep down know that we can do more in this life than just pay our own bills and live our lives entirely for ourselves or anything that serves our interest. There are avenues that glamorize the "I can do whatever I want" lifestyle, and if you believe that, please pause before you get to the end of your life and feel like life cheated you. We can all make a difference through allocating a percentage of our income to a worthy cause and then being committed to that allocation throughout our lives. Once we become responsible and blessed in our finances, we should consider challenging whether in a season of extreme blessing we can give more than we otherwise could.

Recreational Fund

After the giving fund, we continue our budgeting exercise with the recreational fund. If the recreational fund sounds fun, that is because it is fun. The idea behind the recreational fund is that you should put a fixed percentage of your paycheck (not to exceed 5%) toward something fun every two weeks. I believe this is the only fund that should fluctuate. There could be a month where this is only 1%, or even 0%, but I encourage us to try to come up with a fixed percentage and stick with it, as the recreational fund is a motivational tool and helps make budgeting less exhaustive. You can use the recreational fund for something like going out to a nice dinner, a movie, shopping for the pair of shoes that you don't really need, but want so badly, or anything else you can think of that you would consider a bit of a splurge. The possibilities are endless, as it should be something that you enjoy and would find rewarding. One of the things that will keep budgeting attainable and fun is allowing yourself to have the occasional mini-splurge. Every two weeks I always look forward to the recreational fund being refilled. For my wife and I, one of our favorite uses for the recreational fund is to use it to save for vacations. You would be shocked about what type of vacation you could go on in six months if you saved 5% of your paycheck every two weeks.

Life Fund

Lastly, we have the life fund. Essentially, this is what is left over after you have filled up your other funds. The life fund is a true residual or remaining amount, but it is not intended to be used as a "spend at will" fund. My greatest fear is that this becomes the black hole of our budget, where you just make a bunch of purchases and never establish a financial discipline toward budgeting. It is okay to have something left over in the life fund every two weeks (and that is the goal of this budgeting technique) to deposit into your savings fund or as a way to pay off some debt more rapidly. The intent of the life fund is to try and develop a dollar range for the amount of money you have to spend every two weeks on the necessities (food, gas, etc.) and other items that do not fit into the other funds (such as an oil change) so that you can better plan your two weeks. I think it's also important be to very honest with ourselves. If you go buy a luxury couch or handbag because you "need one," you probably are missing the intent of budgeting. If a couch that would fit your needs costs $300, and you want a luxury couch for $1,000, you should take appropriately $700 out of your recreational fund to make this purchase. If you continually have too much left over in your life fund, perhaps you should challenge how much you are allocating up front to your savings or giving funds.

The goal of a well-run life fund is to avoid the situation where you spend, spend, spend and then get ten days into the month only to realize you have no money and feel tempted to dip into the other funds or use a credit card. The life fund sets boundaries, and it should only be tweaked when it is fair to say that too much is being contributed to the other funds (e.g., you are trying to save beyond what you can afford), causing you to have constant shortages in your life fund. In my experience, it is a good idea to track what you are spending through your life fund over a six month period of time. This will give you a pretty good idea of where your money is going. Again, the basic intention is to avoid the life fund becoming a black hole where you spend the rest of your money that is not already in another fund. If you find that a lot of your money in the life fund is being spent on items that are not food, gas, or other basic living needs, it may make sense to challenge whether you are contributing enough to your savings fund. Conversely, you do not want the life fund to be set so low that you struggle to meet your basic needs.

Putting It All Together

An example budget allocation could look like the following for a $2,000 paycheck:

Fund Name	Allocation Method	Amount
Housing	Actual Cost	$450
Savings	10%	$200
Recurring	Actual Cost	$200
Giving	10%	$200
Recreation	5%	$100
Life	Remaining Balance	$850

These are the core funds that I think every budget should include. You can also include other funds for specific purposes as you see fit. For example, I also have an investment fund that helps me separate my cash savings in the savings fund from investment earnings. It is also wise to have a tax fund, which can be contributed to periodically in case you expect to have a tax liability circa April of the next year. It can be a harsh thing to find out in March or April that you have a sizable tax bill and do not have any money earmarked to pay for it. My hope is that this section has given you a tool to use so that you can effectively execute a budget. I use spreadsheets on my computer to track my budget and generally find it to be the best way to execute the budgeting system detailed above. However, as is the truth with any tool, it does not do any good lying in the shed unused. It is still up to you to have the discipline and courage to use this budgeting tool if you want to transform this aspect of your finances from a yearly New Year's resolution to a success story and a new way of life.

Whom To Trust Principles

At this point in the book, hopefully you feel more educated about financial principles and have the motivation to utilize them. In my own experience, the more educated I become in an area, the more questions I inevitably have about those areas. If I know nothing about something, I am going to have a hard time coming up with questions besides, "Tell me about topic X since I have no background on that topic." Once I start to learn the nuances of topic X, I am going to want to ask follow-up questions or do a deeper dive into the topic. Taxes and investments are similar in that they affect all of us and have a lot of depth to them. Once we learn the basics, we want to learn the more advanced aspects as well, because we start to understand how a handle on these areas can have a positive impact on our financial wellbeing.

You could certainly buy a book, like you have here! Sometimes, though, it helps to have a contact that can help discuss these areas with you in person. You certainly want that person to be someone who you think is qualified and trustworthy. With all the bad press about Ponzi schemes and financial advisors being out for "number one," it begs the obvious question: who can you trust? The answer is actually a pretty encouraging one: many people. You just need to seek them out. I love baseball, and one of the things I learned long ago is that you can tell if an umpire is doing a good job by whether the umpire is talked about or not. If an umpire shows up in a press clipping, it is not going to be the following headline: "Joe Umpire called a great game, his strike call in the fifth inning was particularly impressive." No, it does not go that way, does it? More likely would be the following: "Joe Umpire makes controversial strike three call and Atlanta loses the game."

Unfortunately, the media is drawn to negative news. And it is no different in the financial planning realm. You are not going to see a major news channel rave about the financial planner that made ethical decisions for years, thus building a loyal client base. These stories are boring and they have no selling power. But if you are like me, you want a boring story like this when it comes to your finances. I have no interest in being in the news for being a loser in a Ponzi scheme or otherwise. Give me a boring story of a sound financial plan that helps me fund my retirement, and I will be a happy camper. In your search for a financial professional that has pledged to abide by a high standard of care, I introduce to you the CFP®professional, CFA charterholder and CPA.

Professionals with the above distinctions are bound to a strict code of ethics. Those that have CPA licensure, are a CFA charterholder and CFP® professional have all met rigorous requirements wherein ethics are an important cornerstone. In order to continue using these credentials, individuals are required to reemphasize their commitment to a code of ethics through continuing education and signed statements of adherence to an ethical code. In today's environment, where the news has been quick to broadcast major Ponzi schemes, executive greed or financial fraud, hiring individuals with strong ethical values can relieve some of the anxiety. It is also inspiring to see the ethical values that certified practitioners agree to follow.

For example, CFA charterholders abide by a detailed code of ethics that can be viewed on the cfainstitute.org website. It may also be comforting to know that there is also a due diligence requirement for CFA charterholders and CFP® professionals, which requires these individuals to give advice only after researching that advice in good faith. Negligence is neither an option nor acceptable for these professionals. Practitioners are expected to see the warning signs of fraudulent investments and give caution before allowing people to invest in these vehicles. It certainly does not mean that they are going to catch every bad thing that could happen to your finances or know for sure if an investment is fraudulent. However, certified professionals are trained to do enough research about an investment opportunity and to allocate the appropriate level of scrutiny or professional skepticism to it, before recommending it to you. If you ask anyone that has fallen victim to financial fraud, they will probably tell you that having someone on their side that was willing to ask the tough questions would have been well worth the extra price upfront to avoid the financial heartburn on the back end of a bad investment.

The CFP® Professional

With a fee-only CFP® professional you are paying for a financial plan that is tailored to your specific situation. In addition, the CFP® professional can help you carry out that financial plan through regular financial check-ups. This accountability is so invaluable. As a CFP® professional, it is my responsibility to you to come up with a financial plan that works for you, and if it does not initially, I need to find a way to make it happen. A fee-only CFP® professional can give advice that directly impacts you and is not dependent on any products you buy. The CFP® professional is also held to a code of ethics whereby they are obligated to disclose conflicts of interest and independence issues that a client would want to know about before working with that CFP® professional.

Why is a conflict of interest issue a concern? Imagine a scenario where financial planner A has broker buddy B. Financial planner A could go to broker buddy B every time a trade is made for your portfolio. Per se, that seems pretty innocent. However, it is important to be aware that broker buddy B could be charging higher fees than warranted, and only be getting your business because he is friends with financial planner A. Even worse, financial planner A could trade on your account more than necessary in order to generate more brokerage commissions for broker buddy B. Financial planning is so much more than having a great investment portfolio. Paying a transparent fee for an all-inclusive financial plan allows you to feel confident that your advisor is sitting on the same side of the table as you and has a genuine concern for getting you to the right solutions.

How much better would you feel if you knew your financial planner completed a rigorous two-day examination process, met a minimum work experience requirement prior to becoming certified, agreed to adhere to a strict code of ethics and was then required to achieve minimum continuing education to ensure that the professional remains informed in an ever changing financial environment? Most people would agree that this would be fabulous; it is possible by seeking out a CFP® professional. More great news: CFP® professionals are easy to find. The www.cfp.net website offers an excellent search tool that allows you to locate a CFP® professional near you.

Please do not take the above as suggesting that just because someone is a CFP® professional that they are superior to a non-CFP® professional. The discussion is meant to point out the transparency of the qualifications and training of the CFP® professional. You can actually go to www.cfp.net and see the universe of topics on the CFP® exam, which comprise investments, taxes, estate planning, insurance, retirement benefit plans, and other financial planning fundamentals. You can also have comfort that the CFP® professional has pledged to a code of ethics and every two years takes a minimum two hour code of ethics training.

Further, CFP® professional candidates must prove themselves with relevant work experience before becoming certified. This doesn't mean that a CFP® professional is infallible; anyone can make a mistake, but just know that a CFP® professional is at risk of losing their hard earned certification if they willfully give you bad advice or do something else in bad faith. No matter what financial planner you choose, you should inquire into his or her qualifications and the type of training he or she has undergone. Finances can be intimidating to navigate on our own. There are so many things to consider, so it makes perfect sense to reach out to a financial professional to help aid in the process. I can't speak for everyone, but I know that the most important thing for me when giving financial advice is making sure that it's helpful for my clients first. If my clients are not progressing in their financial journey, than I am not doing my job.

The CFA Charterholder

Awareness of the requirements to be a CFA charterholder has steadily risen over the past few years, but there is a long way to go. What matters to us, as individuals looking for help with our financial future, is that CFA charterholders have undergone a difficult program, requiring four years of relevant work experience and passed three separate examinations over a minimum of an eighteen month period, but usually longer. It is hard work. CFA stands for Chartered Financial Analyst®. The program has many relevant topics to the financial planning process. Notably, the CFA program emphasizes ethics, portfolio management, economics and the characteristics of various investment products and strategies. This presents an excellent opportunity for those of you looking for a financial professional who you can trust has undergone vigorous exam requirements (the CFA Institute recommends a minimum of 750 study hours for all three exams combined, but some say it is advisable to study more than 750 hours if one wants to pass). As stated on the cfainstitute.org website, the Chartered Financial Analyst® designation has become the most respected and recognized investment credential in the world.

A CFA charterholder would be very useful for the individual who has a deep desire to work with someone who is very in tune with capital markets and could provide them expertise in the area of asset management. This should be a considerable amount of people, given there are a lot of people that need strong investment returns to have a comfortable retirement. Keeping tabs on financial innovation can be a very difficult process for anyone. CFA charterholders are typically members of local societies that offer the opportunity to have regular access to individuals that are at the forefront of their respective financial fields. Moreover, the CFA Institute does a great job keeping CFA charterholders informed by supplying two bimonthly publications that give up to date developments on global market and economic environments. Having access to a CFA charterholder will allow you to stay informed of the latest market trends, and will provide you with a professional who is trained in understanding retirement portfolio construction and the ongoing maintenance of investment portfolios. Similar to the CFP® professional, you can locate a CFA charterholder on the cfainstitute.org website.

I am impressed by the CFA Institute's Asset Manager Code, which is a requirement for all CFA charterholders to learn, and a standard for which all CFA charterholders are held accountable. The CFA Institute's Asset Manager Code (which is available at www. cfainstitute.org) emphasizes items such as putting client interests first, using prudent judgment in the investment process, and communicating truthfully with clients.

Wouldn't it be a breath of fresh air if you trusted your investment portfolio to a financial professional who had a passion for following the CFA Institute Asset Manager Code principles? Just because there is a CFA Institute Asset Manager Code, doesn't mean that a CFA charterholder will follow it. However, just know that losing CFA charterholder status is not something that I personally would risk for a temporary unethical gain. If you polled my peers, I would be shocked if the majority didn't agree with me.

I am very proud to a member of the CFA Institute. The organization makes it a constant priority to encourage its members to abide by the highest level of ethical standards. Bimonthly I read about stories of CFA Institute members and the CFA Institute board members who try to advocate ways to increase the amount of trust the public can have in the investment markets. It's clear to me that improving the trust that the public has in the investment markets is a core value of the CFA Institute. Can you imagine how comforting it would be to have someone in your corner, managing your investments, who holds this principle as a core value?

The Certified Public Accountant

When most people think of certified public accountants ("CPAs") they probably think of taxes. Though this is not the only thing CPAs are trained to understand, it is a fair generalization as CPAs are able to provide tax advice. The requirements to become a CPA vary by state, but generally each CPA is required to have a certain amount of college hours in accounting, tax or auditing related topics. In addition, to become a CPA, a candidate must pass four separate examinations covering financial accounting, auditing, regulation (tax and legal topics), and other business related topics such as finance and economics; they also are required to engage in continuing education. The broad CPA curriculum provides value to potential clients beyond tax advice. I have frequent conversations with individuals that are surprised that my pursuit of a CPA involved more than just learning about taxes. A CPA should have a basic enough understanding of legal and investment topics to either give you advice or know whom to contact to get an answer to your question. As with the CFP® professional and CFA charterholder, the CPA agrees to adhere to a strict code of ethics.

Online tax software has gotten pretty good, enabling many people with very simple tax situations to navigate through a tax software program without any problems. A CPA is more appropriate for individuals that have the following tax complexities:

- Subject to Alternative Minimum Tax;
- Are an owner in a business;
- Earn income in multiple states;
- Have rental property and
- Actively trade investments.

There are other tax scenarios wherein a trained CPA would prove beneficial as well. The benefit you receive from using a CPA will depend on facts and circumstances, but generally, you will have more peace of mind regarding your taxes with a CPA helping you out. You will also have an advocate, who can assist you with the IRS, should the IRS inquire about a tax position taken on your tax return. I think at a minimum it is advisable to have a CPA contact to call upon if you think you are about to do something that has potential tax implications; if you don't have any idea whether something has tax implications, that is an even better reason to contact a CPA. What takes a CPA five minutes to research, could take the average individual hours to days to research. Your time is too valuable and the risk of taking a faulty tax position is too great; find a local CPA today.

Where Do I Find the Above Professionals?

Finding a listing of individuals with the above designations is pretty straightforward. A listing of individuals with the CFP® certification is located at www.cfp.net. The website allows you to search by city and state or zip code. Locating a CFA charterholder is a similar process, via the following url: www.cfainstitute.org. As a CPA must be licensed with a state, finding a CPA in your residency will require going to your state's secretary of state website.

In Summary

The key point is that you need to know what qualifies your financial professional to give you financial planning advice. Just having a certification does not make someone a superior financial planner. However, you can at least trust that certified financial professionals have made a commitment to high standards and show a certain level of competency by completing a difficult program. Personally, that is why I am proud to be affiliated with the above organizations.

If you follow sports, you may have heard accounts of professional athletes who go broke in part because they received financial advice from someone who was just trying to exploit the professional athlete. It's a cautionary tale that you need to be careful of when you shop for financial services. Consider this; would you be better off if your financial planner only benefited when they provided you a financial plan and a sound support system that you could have confidence in and got real results? I have a deep passion for the financial services industry. It is why I pursued the career I did. I saw an opportunity to make things better for individuals who had plenty of financial questions but were not sure where to go for financial answers. There are many others just like me out there who would love to help you move closer to your financial dreams. Where are you going to go with your next financial question?

Estate Planning Principles

Up until this point, a lot of our discussion has been about how to manage your finances in the present moment. There will come a time however when the focus will be not on how to accumulate further wealth, but rather on how to distribute that wealth. As you can imagine, distributing your wealth can be a complex topic, and one that it is worth paying the money to seek legal counsel to ensure you get it right. We work so hard our entire lives and thus deserve the peace of mind that our money and our possessions will move on to the right people or organizations, rather than being stuck in some courthouse battle for a period of time.

It is easy to immediately think, "This section does not apply to me. I am barely getting by as it is, and just I hope I can retire." The reason this section does apply, though, is because of probate. Probate is the process in which the courts decide where everything you possess goes once you die. It is a process whereby a will is interpreted and then a judge makes a decision on all of your "stuff." There is some risk that the probate process will not decide to distribute your assets when you die in the exact manner you intended or in the most efficient manner possible. There are some ways to avoid the probate process, which I will discuss later in this section. Common probate avoidance vehicles are trusts and life insurance plans.

Estate Tax and the Power of Gifting Strategies

The estate tax is not something everyone faces and can depend entirely on the year you die, since the estate tax limits vary from year to year and can change quickly at the stroke of a legislative pen. This section will cover some of the basics of a complex topic: federal estate taxation.

An estate tax in its simplest context is a tax on all the assets you own when you die. Your estate is all the property you own, such as your money, investments and real property (but not limited to these).

Before assets go to your heirs, these assets will need to be evaluated for estate tax purposes, and if all or a part of the asset requires estate tax, it will become due before your heir can collect the item (whoever files your estate tax return will pay the tax). When the asset is cash, this isn't as complicated. For instance, if I leave $10,000 for my heir and my estate gets taxed at 40% (this is in line with current guidance, but estate tax rates change frequently and have been as high as 55% in the past), my heir will ultimately just receive $6,000 after $4,000 in estate taxes are paid. 40% is actually the top tax rate at which an estate would be assessed. Estate taxes are calculated using a graduated tax structure, but I'll assume 40% throughout this section for simplicity's sake. Imagine if an heir receives a $100,000 house and there is a tax of $40,000 on it. First the estate will be liable to pay the $40,000 in tax. If the tax is not paid by the estate, the heir will need to remit $40,000 in cash! You can see how this creates a problem, as $40,000 in immediate cash is not something we all necessarily have sitting in a bank account, and the estate may not have that amount in cash either. This could cause the heir to take a loan or sell the house to pay for the estate tax.

Luckily, there are two relief measures that prevent estates (or their heirs if the estate cannot afford the taxes) from being taxed, and a few other tax planning strategies that can be used, such as using gifts, trusts, and life insurance.

The first relief measure is the marital exclusion. What this means is that if I die, I can give everything in my name to my wife, tax-free. It is not until my wife dies that my possessions will face estate tax. Secondly, there is an exclusion amount, and in some years the exclusion amount is quite high. In 2013, any estate worth $5,250,000 or less avoids estate tax. If your estate is worth $5,350,000, the estate would pay tax on the excess, or $100,000. In addition, exclusions are portable between spouses, so if the first deceased spouse left all of their estate to the surviving spouse (and thus did not use any of their ($5,250,000 exclusion amount), the surviving spouse would have an exclusion amount of over $10,000,000. Having an exclusion amount of $5,250,000 is helpful from an estate tax perspective because an estate of $5,250,000 is quite large and will allow many to avoid estate taxation. This doesn't mean we should ignore estate taxation. Estate tax exclusion limits have varied over the years and could be much lower in future years. In addition, our personal wealth could be much higher in the future.

From a strategic perspective, you can avoid some estate tax by making annual cash gifts of up to $14,000 to anyone of your choosing. Any cash gifts over $14,000 to an individual in a given year lower the amount of your estate tax exclusion and could eventually be subject to a gift tax of 40% which is strategically similar to the estate tax rate of 40%. The gift tax is in place so that someone does not give $100,000 to their son a few years before death to avoid estate tax on that $100,000. However, gifting can be a helpful way to lower the value of an estate.

For instance, if you have two children, you can give them a gift each year of $14,000 for 10 years and neither they nor your estate will pay tax on that exchange. If you were to wait until you died and then gave each of your children $140,000, there is the possibility that there would be estate tax of 40% on each $140,000 payment, leaving your heirs with $84,000 instead. This isn't the most efficient outcome, because the $140,000 has already been taxed once during your lifetime and is then being taxed again before it is left to your heirs. There are attorneys that specialize in this area that will be able to help you plan if you think you are going to face an estate tax issue. Most financial professionals will have contacts with an estate planning professional and be able to coordinate on your behalf, which is great for you, because this can be a complex and time consuming planning process to do alone.

Another way to lower the value of your estate at death, and thus the related estate tax, is through the use of trusts. A common estate tax planning theme is coming up with ways to get assets out of your estate before death, so that when you die, your estate will not be assessed the estate tax on as many assets. The following section is a brief discussion on trusts, which should give you enough information to know what trusts are and when you may need to use a trust. Setting one up will likely require an attorney.

Revocable Trust vs. Irrevocable Trust

A trust can be a very useful mechanism for distributing your wealth to your beneficiaries in a controlled manner. A trust will have a trustee that will charge the trust fees to manage the assets and perform other administrative functions, such as tracking when to distribute wealth, distributing the wealth to your beneficiaries, etc. The trustee is able to invest the assets you put in the trust in line with a specific objective that you communicate. For example, if you want the trustee to focus on maintaining principal (the initial amount you put in the trust) and make most of the distributions between a 10 year and 30 year window from when the trust was opened, the trustee can invest in fixed income investments with expected maturities between 10 and 30 years. Of course, they could also invest in stocks and sell them at the appropriate times to make the required payments to your beneficiaries. The way it is done is up to you or can be decided by the trustee (who is held to a fiduciary standard of care). The trust is also good because it provides some discipline to the process of distributing your wealth. Likely you have worked very hard to accumulate your wealth, so you would want that wealth to be spent by your beneficiaries in a responsible manner. A trust can be designed to distribute money over time, like an annuity, rather than a lump sum of money at one time. Further, the trust can put limits on the beneficiary's rights to the trust's assets until they reach a certain age. These two features try to mitigate the risk that a young beneficiary will receive a lot of money at once and make irresponsible decisions.

When deciding on a trust, there are two types to consider. The two types of trusts available to you are the revocable and irrevocable (or as I like to say changeable or unchangeable) trusts. The difference between the two mainly relates to who has the power over the assets. In a revocable trust, the person who decides to set up the trust can change the nature of the trust after it is set up. This can be things like changing the beneficiaries or even in some cases canceling the trust altogether. This type of trust gives the grantor (or starter) of the trust more power, but for tax purposes the grantor of the trust is considered to be in ownership of the trust assets and must pay taxes on the trust income. Also, the trust assets get brought into the calculation of the estate at death and thus face estate tax. This is an obvious disadvantage of the revocable trust, as a trust can be a useful mechanism for an individual to lower an estate tax liability.

Conversely, an irrevocable trust is a legal transfer of assets from the grantor to the trustee. As the name suggests, the grantor no longer has the ability to control the assets and thus does not pay taxes on the income of the trust, nor need to consider these assets for purposes of calculating the estate tax liability. The trust gets the tax bill and the trustee is responsible for paying the taxes using the assets in the trust. These are the two major positives of this type of trust, so if controlling the assets is not a desire for the grantor, this would be a highly recommended option. Having a revocable trust (and thus maintaining the power to control the trust assets) is useful when there is not absolute certainty about your intended beneficiaries.

Life Insurance

If you have watched a lot of sports like me, it is likely you have been inundated with life insurance commercials. I can't speak for some of the other television programming, but it wouldn't shock me if life insurance commercials show up on other standard cable channels as well. Life insurance is something you buy if you want to protect your loved ones in case you pass away. It is insurance that you buy on your income producing ability, so that if you die, that income flow will continue to your loved ones. It is understandably a sensitive topic, as I rarely run into people that would like to openly talk about preparing for their death. This section hits the highlights on life insurance, but the product universe is diverse and can be complicated. If you think you are ready to purchase life insurance, a life insurance representative should be able to provide you with the necessary information to pick the right policy for your particular situation. My goal is simply to raise awareness of life insurance's role in a financial plan and hopefully make you feel a bit more educated on the topic. As alluded to earlier, you can take money out of your savings and use it to buy life insurance. This is a way for your assets to escape estate tax and probate because life insurance will be in the name of whomever you decide and thus will not be subject to a probate court decision. I view this as a major advantage in favor of life insurance.

Life insurance has an escalating cost because it is cheapest when you are young (and don't always foresee a need for it given you may not have a beneficiary to protect) and gradually increases in cost as you age (at the time you start thinking about what your beneficiaries would do in the event of your death). I think this illustrates the importance of planning early. A married couple without kids, that both work, probably does not need to be tremendously concerned with life insurance, as it's likely that in the event one of them dies, the needs of the household will be cut in half. However, if a couple starts thinking about having children, it could make sense at that point to start buying life insurance, even as soon as the baby arrives. I say this because the possibility of locking in lower life insurance premiums (a fancy word for the amount you pay the life insurance company each month to continue to have life insurance) is an attractive option if you know life insurance is already going to be a part of your future.

There are two general types: whole life (sometimes referred to as cash value) and term. Whole life is pretty easy to remember, because the concept is straightforward: you pay life insurance policy premiums your whole life (in its most simple form, the payments are level and continuous), and when you pass away, your assigned beneficiaries are given a certain amount of money stated in your life insurance policy.

The benefit of the whole life policy is the confidence in knowing your payment schedule in advance and not having to worry about renewing your policy as you age and premium payments escalate. You also build up a cash value portion that increases tax-free, which is a tax efficient way to save for the future. With a whole life insurance policy, it does not matter when you die — your beneficiary will still receive the amount stated on the policy as long as premiums have been paid as agreed upon. Within the whole life policy family there are variations such as variable life, universal life and variable universal life. These enhancements to the standard whole life policy are available if you want some variability in your premium payments or want to take advantage of different types of investment offerings. In all likelihood your premiums and fees will be much higher with a whole life insurance policy.

Conversely, the term life insurance policy is for a term or period of your life. If you die within the term of the life insurance policy, your beneficiaries are paid the face value of the life insurance policy. However, if you die after the period ends, your beneficiaries will not receive the stated value on the life insurance policy.

Term life insurance premiums are lower than whole life premiums because the period of coverage is shorter and you aren't trying to build up a cash value. These policies have the obvious downside of not producing a benefit to your beneficiaries if your term ends while you are still alive, but insurance doesn't always produce a benefit, such as when you have car insurance but never wreck your car. I tend to favor term life policies because you pay the minimum it takes to ensure the protection of your income earning ability. Ideally, you will be saving for retirement through some other tax efficient vehicle like an IRA or 401(k) and won't get as much use out of the extra premiums paid toward the cash value portion of a whole life policy. Life insurance is a risk management tool and as such it makes the most sense to me as protection toward the loss of one's future income producing ability, not as an investment vehicle.

When a beneficiary begins to receive payments, they will have the option of receiving installment payments or a lump sum payment. A neat benefit of life insurance payments is that they are not taxable to the recipient if the lump sum option is used. The installment option allows the recipient to receive payments over time, with the principal or portions of principal remaining with the insurance company, earning interest. The earned interest on the life insurance policy is taxable to the recipient. Some people prefer the annuity because it gives them a constant stream of income and has a built in discipline mechanism that requires the recipient to live within their means. The lump sum payment has the benefit of being received at once, tax-free, so that it could theoretically be invested in a vehicle that will earn more income than the money would if it remained with the insurance company. Life insurance can be a complicated topic and there are many nuances that I did not discuss in this section. A life insurance representative will be able to provide you a nice summary of each life insurance type, and the variations you can make to each type, before you make your decision.

Alternative Wealth Transfer Vehicles

There are also other wealth transfer vehicles to consider, such as a private foundation, which can serve to provide a tax efficient mechanism to transfer wealth for a specific cause. If you are considering a private foundation, legal counsel is recommended to ensure you are able to accomplish both the charitable purposes and get the desired tax benefits.

In summary, your wealth transference strategy should accomplish two goals: your wealth should reach the intended beneficiaries in the timeliest fashion possible (avoid probate) and be done in the most tax efficient way possible so as to maximize the amount of money transferred to your intended beneficiaries. Thinking about how you are going to give your possessions to your beneficiaries is not the most positive or energizing topic, but it is to your advantage to start planning early. It is very easy to procrastinate in this area because it deals with an uncomfortable personal topic, which of course is our own mortality. Try to overcome thinking about yourself and instead shift the focus to the impact your estate planning will have on your loved ones or favorite cause(s). For a lot of you, the people you are leaving your assets to at death happen to also be the very same people you are working to provide for at this very moment. This area is complex and is not an area where we should give the minimum effort. My three favorite words in this area are consult, consult, and consult. If there is one thing that is worth paying a lawyer or CFP® professional to do, it would be getting their help with proper estate planning.

Conclusion

Congratulations on completing your journey through this book. I can certainly relate to the challenge of paying the money to buy a book (I am eternally grateful for you by the way) and finding time to read it amid a very busy schedule. It is so hard to sit down and read a book, with the numerous distractions available to us! This book was intended to serve as both a reference resource for you and as a motivational tool. By buying this book and reading it, you have already accomplished the first step in having an exciting financial future; you are taking the initiative to seek information that can equip you with an improved financial perspective. It is my prayer (and yes I pray for the readers of this book) that you will now form different financial habits. Now that you have this knowledge, you will be empowered if you apply it.

A lot of the financial failures I see are attributable to individuals not taking their financial future seriously enough and instead opting to live day to day and hoping for the best. That is not the plight for the readers of this book. You now have ten financial principles that have raised your financial awareness and if you follow them diligently, you will find yourself in a position whereby you are achieving better financial results than you would have otherwise. You are already so much further along than most people because you had the discipline to read a short book on how to improve your financial future. You no doubt have a new found seriousness toward your finances and hopefully much more confidence than you did before you read this book. You will also find that the same discipline that you develop to succeed in your finances will also spill over into the other areas of your life. My prayer is that we become more disciplined employees and employers, fathers and mothers, brothers and sisters, sons and daughters.

Now that you have read this book once, I advise you to keep it around as a handy reference guide. There is so much information in this book that it is hard to remember it all after one pass. I have read some of my favorite books three or more times, and each time I read those books, I pick up an insight that I did not receive my previous time through the book. If you want to set up a budget (and I know you want to, and will!), it will undoubtedly help to revisit this book to make sure you have made all the considerations for how to set up a budget template that will work for you. You may want to revisit this book during tax season to recall some of the common before and after AGI tax deductions. Do not try to do this all by yourself. The financial world can be a scary place, but there are plenty of financial professionals out there that are smart, ethical, and willing to help you pursue your financial dreams. These are just a few ideas, and I encourage you to come up with your own uses for this book, as therein lays its intent: to give every reader an idea or concept that will change their financial future forever.

About the Author

James Giuliani is a CFA® charterholder, CFP$_1$® professional, and CPA residing in Atlanta, Georgia. He has a BBA in accounting from Emory University and has spent his entire professional career in the financial services industry. He is married to the former Angela Davie and has one son, Jonah Matthew. When not working he can be found spending time with family and friends, reading, exercising, and watching sports.

[1]Certified Financial Planner Board of Standards Inc. owns the certification marks CFP®, Certified Financial Planner™ and federally registered CFP (with flame design) in the U.S., which it awards to individuals who successfully complete CFP Board's initial and ongoing certification requirements.